Certified SOLIDWORKS Expert
Preparation Materials

SOLIDWORKS 2017

Written by: Sr. Certified SOLIDWORKS Instructor

Paul Tran, CSWE, CSWI

SDC Publications
P.O. Box 1334
Mission, KS 66222
913-262-2664
www.SDCpublications.com
Publisher: Stephen Schroff

Copyright 2016 Paul Tran

The lessons and exercises in this textbook are the sole property of the author. The material is to be used for learning purposes only and not to be used in any way deleterious to the interest of the author.

This textbook is copyrighted and the author reserves all rights. No part of this publication may be reproduced, transmitted, transcribed, stored in a retrieval system or translated into any language or computer language, in any form or by any means, electronic, mechanical magnetic, optical, chemical, manual, or otherwise, without the prior written permission from the author.

It is a violation of United States copyright laws to make copies in any form or media of the contents of this book for commercial or educational purposes without written permission.

Examination Copies
Books received as examination copies are for review purposes only and may not be made available for student use. Resale of examination copies is prohibited.

Electronic Files
Any electronic files associated with this book are licensed to the original user only. These files may not be transferred to any other party.

Trademarks
SOLIDWORKS is a registered trademark of Dassault Systems. Microsoft Excel / Word are registered trademarks of Microsoft Corporation. All other brand names or trademarks belong to their respective companies.

Disclaimer
The author makes a sincere effort to ensure the accuracy of the material described herein, however the author makes no warranty, expressed or implied, with respect to the quality, correctness, reliability, currency, accuracy, or freedom from error of this document or the products it describes.

The author disclaims all liability for any direct, indirect, incidental or consequential, special or exemplary damages resulting from the use of the information in this document or from the use of any products described in this document. Data used in examples and sample data files are intended to be fictional.

ISBN-13: 978-1-60357-065-7
ISBN-10: 1-63057-065-9

Printed and bound in the United States of America.

Acknowledgments

Thanks as always to my wife Vivian for always being there and providing support and honest feedback on all the chapters in the textbook. I would like to give a special thanks to Karla Werner and Rachel Schroff for their editing and corrections. Additionally thanks to Kevin Douglas for writing the foreword.

I also have to thank SDC Publications and the staff for its continuing encouragement and support for this edition of the **CSWE SOLIDWORKS Certified Expert Preparation Materials** and special thanks to Zach Werner for putting together such beautiful cover design

Finally, I would like to thank you, our readers, for your continued support. It is with your consistent feedback that we were able to create the lessons and exercises in this book with more detailed and useful information.

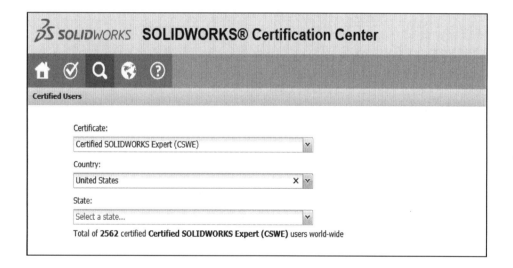

CSWE - Certified SOLIDWORKS Expert

A Certified SOLIDWORKS Expert is someone who easily demonstrates the ability to utilize advanced functions and features to solve complex modeling challenges.

A CSWE will be well rounded in their knowledge of all areas of the SOLIDWORKS software. A CSWE is able to solve practically any modeling problem given to them, and is traditionally the go-to SOLIDWORKS user among their colleagues.

Exam Prerequisites:
To qualify to take the CSWE exam, a candidate must have:
- Successfully passed the CSWP exam.
- Successfully passed Four advanced topic exams such as:

CSWP-Sheet Metal, CSWP-Mold, CSWP-Surfaces, CSWP-Weldments, and CSWP-Advanced Drawings.

The CSWE exam is meant to be the most challenging exam SOLIDWORKS has to offer, so therefore no sample exam is provided. If the exam is not successfully passed, you will have to wait 180 days to retake the exam.

Exam Length: 4 hours
SOLIDWORKS 2015 or later is required to take the exam.

Minimum Passing grade: 80%
All candidates receive electronic certificates, business card logos and personal listing on CSWP-CSWE directories when they pass.

Exam may feature hands-on challenges in some of these areas:
- Lofts
- Sweeps
- In-context assembly changes
- Imported part modifications
- Belts and chains
- Sketch blocks
- Multi-bodies
- In-context assembly design
- Advanced Weldments
- Curved Spring modeling
- Move/Copy bodies
- Advanced Sheet metal
- Surfaces

This text will guide you through the best practices when working with those challenges.

Foreword

While serving on the executive management team at US CAD, a large Autodesk and soon to be SOLIDWORKS VAR based in southern California, I had the good fortune of meeting an up and coming CAD Instructor, Paul Tran in the mid-1990s as a revolutionary, PC-based, 3D mechanical design technology was beginning to make its way into the marketplace – SOLIDWORKS was born.

Shortly thereafter, Paul began regularly teaching the SOLIDWORKS courses for local designers & engineers eager to learn what appeared to be market-changing technology. Speaking with many students from a wide variety of industries after their courses with Paul revealed a common theme – they universally loved the class, the Instructor and SOLIDWORKS! It was clear that we had landed someone special in the world of educating others, someone with a true passion to teach.

Fast forward almost 20 years later with thousands of students taught and a common theme continues to emerge from students from all of Paul's classes – they loved the class, the Instructor and SOLIDWORKS! What has made Paul such a successful educator of SOLIDWORKS technology, is that even after hundreds of courses taught, he approaches each new class as if it were his first: Excited to teach new designers SOLIDWORKS for the first time. Working patiently with students at all design skill levels. Passionate about former students coming in for advanced skills development.

Paul's latest book, CSWE is the ideal preparatory tutorial for those designers and engineers who have the desire to become the best of the best SOLIDWORKS users in the world and claim the official title of "Certified SOLIDWORKS Expert." In today's hyper-competitive business world, mechanical design professionals that carry the SOLIDWORKS Expert certification hold a distinct advantage over their peers - an advantage that can bring many more job opportunities, greater career advancement, higher incomes and increased job satisfaction. The CSWE Program is a rigorous examination that requires thorough preparation to help ensure a successful outcome. Paul's extensive experience prepping hundreds of users to become Certified SOLIDWORKS Professionals (CSWP) and his continued drive to provide SOLIDWORKS professionals with the best instructional tools and methods will make The CSWE guide a must-have for those who seek to sit at the top of their trade.

Kevin Douglas
Vice President Sales/Board of Advisors, GoEngineer

Author's Note

CSWE - Certified SOLIDWORKS Expert - Preparation Materials is comprised of lessons based on the feedback from Paul's former CSWEs students and engineering professionals. Paul has 30 years of experience in the fields of mechanical and manufacturing engineering; 20 years were in teaching and supporting the SOLIDWORKS software and its add-ins. As an active Sr. SOLIDWORKS instructor and design engineer, Paul has worked and consulted with hundreds of reputable companies including; IBM, Intel, NASA, US-Navy, Boeing, Disneyland, Medtronic, Oakley, Kingston, Community Colleges, Universities, and many others. Today, he has trained nearly 9,000 engineering professionals, and given guidance to half of the number of Certified SOLIDWORKS Professionals and Certified SOLIDWORKS Expert (CSWP & CSWE) in the state of California.

Every lesson in this book was created based on the actual CSWE Examination. Each of these projects have been broken down and developed into easy and comprehendible steps for the reader. Furthermore, every challenge is explained very clearly in short chapters, ranging from 10 to 20 pages. Each and every single step comes with the exact screen shot to help you understand the main concept of each design more easily. Learn the CSWE Preparation materials at your own pace, as you progress from Parts to Assemblies, and then to more complex design challenges.

About the Training Files

The files for this textbook are available for download on the publisher's website at www.SDCpublications.com/downloads/978-1-63057-067-5. They are organized by the chapter numbers and the file names that are normally mentioned at the beginning of each chapter or exercise. In the Completed Parts folder you will also find copies of the parts, assemblies and drawings that were created for cross references or reviewing purposes.

It would be best to make a copy of the content to your local hard drive and work from these documents; you can always go back to the original training files location at anytime in the future, if needed.

Who this book is for

This book was written for the advanced users and those who have already accomplished the CSWP title, and those who are already familiar with the SOLIDWORKS program and its add-ins. It is also a great resource for the more CAD literate individuals who want to expand their knowledge of the different features that SOLIDWORKS has to offer. The lessons and exercises are intended to assist you in familiarizing yourself with the structures of the exams and the method in which the questions are asked.

The organization of the book

The chapters in this book are organized in the logical order in which you would learn the SOLIDWORKS CSWE exam preparation materials. Each chapter will guide you through some different tasks, from part modifications, to some advanced Multibody Parts modeling, Top Down Assemblies, Surfaces and move on to more complex tasks that are common to all SOLIDWORKS releases.

The conventions in this book

This book uses the following conventions to describe the actions you perform when using the keyboard and mouse to work in SOLIDWORKS:

Click: means to press and release the mouse button. A click of a mouse button is used to select a command or an item on the screen.

Double Click: means to quickly press and release the left mouse button twice. A double mouse click is used to open a program, or show the dimensions of a feature.

Right Click: means to press and release the right mouse button. A right mouse click is used to display a list of commands, a list of shortcuts that is related to the selected item.

Click and Drag: means to position the mouse cursor over an item on the screen and then press and hold down the left mouse button; still holding down the left button, move the mouse to the new destination and release the mouse button. Drag and drop makes it easy to move things around within a SOLIDWORKS document.

Bolded words: indicated the action items that you need to perform.

Italic words: Side notes and tips that give you additional information, or to explain special conditions that may occur during the course of the task.

Numbered Steps: indicates that you should follow these steps in order to successfully perform the task.

Icons: indicates the buttons or commands that you need to press.

SOLIDWORKS 2017

SOLIDWORKS is program suite, or a collection of engineering programs that can help you design better products faster. SOLIDWORKS contains different combinations of programs; some of the programs used in this book may not be available in your suites.

Start and exit SOLIDWORKS

SOLIDWORKS allows you to start its program in several ways. You can either double click on its shortcut icon on the desktop, or go to the Start menu and select the following: All Program / SOLIDWORKS, or drag a SOLIDWORKS document and drop it on the SOLIDWORKS shortcut icon.

Before exiting SOLIDWORKS, be sure to save any open documents, and then click File / Exit; you can also click the X button on the top right of your screen to exit the program.

Using the Toolbars

You can use toolbars to select commands in SOLIDWORKS rather than using the drop down menus. Using the toolbars is normally faster. The toolbars come with commonly used commands in SOLIDWORKS, but they can be customized to help you work more efficiently.

To access the toolbars, either right click in an empty spot on the top right of your screen or select View / Toolbars.

To customize the toolbars, select Tools / Customize. When the dialog pops up, click on the Commands tab, select a Category, and then drag an icon out of the dialog box and drop it on a toolbar that you want to customize. To remove an icon from a toolbar, drag an icon out of the toolbar and drop it into the dialog box.

Using the task pane

The task pane is normally kept on the right side of your screen. It display various options like SOLIDWORKS resources, Design library, File explorer, Search, View palette, Appearances and Scenes, Custom properties, Built-in libraries, Technical alerts and news, etc,.

The task pane provides quick access to any of the mentioned items by offering the drag and drop function to all of its contents. You can see a large preview of a SOLIDWORKS document before opening it. New documents can be saved in the task pane at anytime, and existing documents can also be edited and re-saved. The task pane can be resized, close or move to different location on your screen if needed.

Table of Contents

Introduction:	**Are You the Next CSWE?**	
Chapter 1:	**Using Belt Chain**	**1-1**
	Chapter summary	1-1
	Tools Needed	1-2
	Staring a new part template	1-3
	Creating the main sketch	1-3
	Making the blocks	1-4
	Creating a belt chain	1-5
	Entering the belt length	1-6
	Adding the angular dimensions	1-7
	Applying dimension changes	1-8
	Checking the belt length	1-9
	Changing the pulley's angle	1-9
	Verifying the new belt length	1-10
	Exercise: Creating a Belt Chain	1-11
Chapter 2:	**Advanced Weldments**	**2-1**
	Chapter summary	2-1
	Tools Needed	2-2
	Starting a new part template	2-3
	Creating a 3D sketch	2-3
	Creating the second portion of the 3D sketch	2-6
	Connecting the sketch entities	2-7
	Adding the structural members	2-8
	Assigning the material	2-9
	Calculating the mass	2-10
	Adding more groups	2-11
	Calculating the mass	2-12
	Modifying the dimensions	2-13
	Calculating the mass	2-14
Chapter 3:	**Advanced Sheet Metal**	**3-1**
	Chapter summary	3-1
	Tools Needed	3-2
	Opening an IGES document	3-3
	Changing the display style	3-4

	Enabling the Sheet Metal tool tab	3-5
	Converting to sheet metal	3-5
	Measuring the flat length	3-6
	Unfolding the bends	3-7
	Extruding a cut	3-8
	Folding the bends	3-8
	Assigning material	3-9
	Calculating the mass	3-9

Chapter 4: Cam Motions — 4-1

	Chapter summary	4-1
	Tools Needed	4-2
	Opening an assembly document	4-3
	Adding a tangent mate	4-4
	Measuring the minimum distance	4-5
	Measuring the maximum distance	4-6

Chapter 5: Assembly Drawings & BOMs — 5-1

	Chapter summary	5-1
	Tools Needed	5-2
	Opening an assembly document	5-3
	Transferring to a drawing	5-4
	Adding an isometric drawing view	5-5
	Adding a Bill of Materials	5-6
	Changing the column property	5-7
	Locating the quantity	5-7
	Creating another custom property	5-7
	Locating the Finish	5-8
	Changing the BOM Type	5-9
	Locating the sub-components	5-9

Chapter 6: Assembly Modifications — 6-1

	Chapter summary	6-1
	Tools Needed	6-2
	Opening an assembly document	6-3
	Creating a new plane	6-3
	Creating a new component	6-4
	Creating a Fit Spline	6-6
	Creating a new plane	6-7
	Sketching the sweep profile	6-7
	Creating the sweep	6-8
	Assigning material	6-9

| | Calculating the mass | 6-9 |

Chapter 7: **Combine Common** **7-1**
	Chapter summary	7-1
	Tools Needed	7-2
	Using Combine common Part 1	7-8
	Starting a new part document	7-3
	Creating the first solid body	7-3
	Creating the second solid body	7-5
	Creating a combine-command body	7-6
	Finding the volume of the new body	7-7
	Using Combine common Part 2	7-8
	Starting a new part document	7-8
	Creating the first solid body	7-8
	Creating the second solid body	7-10
	Creating a combine-common body	7-11
	Finding the volume of the new body	7-12
	Using Combine common Part 3	7-13
	Opening a part document	7-13
	Adding an Angle and Depth chamfer	7-14
	Changing to a Distance and Distance chamfer	7-14
	Creating an Offset Face chamfer	7-15
	Changing to a Face-Face chamfer	7-15
	Creating a Split Line	7-16
	Creating a Parting Line Draft	7-17
	Assigning material	7-18
	Calculating the mass	7-18

Chapter 8: **Part Modifications** **8-1**
	Chapter summary	8-1
	Tools Needed	8-2
	Part Modification – Challenge 1 of 5	8-3
	Opening a part document	8-3
	Modifying the pattern angle	8-4
	Changing the pattern angle	8-5
	Calculating the final mass	8-5
	Part Modification – Challenge 2 of 5	8-6
	Opening a part document	8-6
	Filling the hollow cavity	8-7
	Deleting the first group of fillets	8-8
	Removing the second group of fillets	8-9
	Removing the third group of fillets	8-10
	Modifying the base	8-11

	Removing the outer portion	8-12
	Adding fillets to the base	8-14
	Adding fillets to other features	8-14
	Shelling the part	8-15
	Creating a section view	8-15
	Assigning material	8-16
	Calculating the final mass	8-17
	Part Modification – Challenge 3 of 5	8-18
	Opening a part document	8-18
	Creating a cut feature	8-19
	Creating a Circular Pattern of the body	8-20
	Assigning material	8-21
	Calculating the final mass	8-21
	Part Modification – Challenge 4 of 5	8-22
	Opening a part document	8-22
	Converting the outline of the pattern	8-22
	Removing the raised pattern	8-24
	Extruding a cut	8-24
	Creating the sweep path	8-25
	Creating a swept feature	8-26
	Calculating the mass	8-27
	Part Modification – Challenge 5 of 5	8-29
	Opening a part document	8-29
	Creating an onset surface	8-29
	Creating a surface fill	8-30
	Creating a lofted feature	8-30
	Creating the new cut profile	8-31
	Creating fillets	8-32
Chapter 9:	**Cut with Surface**	**9-1**
	Chapter summary	9-1
	Tools Needed	9-2
	Opening an assembly file	9-3
	Editing the PartB	9-3
	Creating an offset surface	9-4
	Creating a surface cut	9-5
	Hiding a component	9-6
	Hiding a surface	9-6
	Removing the sharp edges	9-7
	Exiting the edit part mode	9-8
	Calculating the mass	9-8
	Exercise: Cut with Surface	9-9

Chapter 10:	**Creating a Curved Spring**	**10-1**
	Chapter summary	10-1
	Tools Needed	10-2
	Starting a new part	10-3
	Creating the sweep path	10-3
	Creating the sweep profile	10-4
	Creating a swept feature	10-4
	Assigning material	10-5
	Calculating the mass	10-6
	Exercise: Circular Spring	10-7
	Spring Examples	10-10
Chapter 11:	**Surface Modifications**	**11-1**
	Chapter summary	11-1
	Tools Needed	11-2
	Opening a part document	11-3
	Deleting the faces of the model	11-3
	Measuring the current angle	11-4
	Rotating the handle	11-5
	Recreating the deleted surfaces	11-6
	Hiding a surface body	11-8
	Trimming surfaces	11-9
	Showing a surface body	11-10
	Knitting all surface bodies	11-10
	Creating a section view	11-11
	Measuring the mass	11-11

Glossary
Index
Quick-Guide

Are You the Next CSWE?

A Certified SOLIDWORKS Expert (CSWE) is someone who easily demonstrates the ability to utilize advanced functions and features to solve complex modeling challenges.

A CSWE will be well rounded in their knowledge of all areas of the SOLIDWORKS software. A CSWE is able to solve practically any modeling problem given to them, and is traditionally the go-to SOLIDWORKS user among their colleagues.

The modeling challenges in the examination will test your ability to select the correct functions to use and solve each problem. It expects you to know how to best use most of the commands, and combine them to get to the solution. The SOLIDWORKS software is powerful enough to assist you with solving most of the 3D design issues using various methods, but as a CSWE, you should know the best method to solve it, and solve it quickly.

At the time of this writing, there are 62,288 Certified SOLIDWORKS Professionals (CSWP) worldwide, but only 2,562 CSWE around the world.

According to some of the experts who have already taken the CSWE exam, it is difficult and somewhat stressful, but with some preparation is it manageable. The CSWE Certification is ranked as the highest certification that SOLIDWORKS has to offer. It is a great achievement that is highly respected. Ultimately, the people that set their goals to achieve the CSWE Certification are the power users or the SOLIDWORKS guru as some people would call it.

The exam is priced at $149.00 USD and consists of 10 different design challenges that spread out to 20 questions such as: Solid / Surface Modifications, Top-Down Assembly, Assembly Mates, External References, Multibody Parts and Belt Chain Blocks. All must be completed within the allowed four hour time frame. Unlike the CSWP exam, there are no multiple choice questions in this exam, therefore you will not be able to determine whether your answers are correct until the exam has been completed and graded.

Though the style is somewhat similar to the CSWP exam, it is much more complex and it requires a much broader understanding of all areas of the SOLIDWORKS software in order to solve the challenges and determine the best solutions; this book was designed to guide you through some of the best practices for solving these types of issues.

The author recommends that you work with the lessons in this book at least three to five times, and then time yourself and to see if you can complete all ten challenges within four hours before attempting to take the actual CSWE exam.

Not only is your time very valuable, but if you fail, the waiting time for re-take is six months, and of course, you would have to pay the $149.00 exam fees again. So ultimately, let's study hard and pass this highest-ranked certification on your very first try!

CSWE Certification Home Page:
http://www.SOLIDWORKS.com/sw/support/CSWE.htm

CSWE Sample Certificate

CHAPTER 1

Using Belt Chain

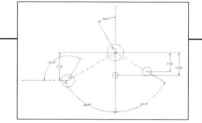

CSWE Exam Preparation
Using Belt Chain

Belt / Chain is one of the unique features in SOLIDWORKS for designing sprockets, belts and pulleys.

The pulleys are created as a single sketch and converted into blocks. They get positioned with relations and dimensions, then a belt is added and its length is determined by the pulleys positions.

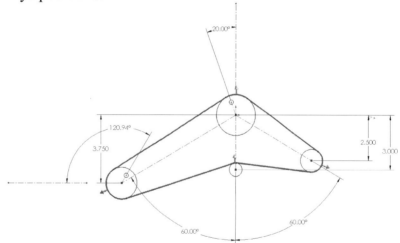

Depending on the location of the pulleys, SOLIDWORKS calculates the length for the belt automatically. Once the belt is created, the belt length can be altered and the pulleys are adjusted accordingly.

This chapter will guide you through the creation of the pulley system shown above. Four blocks will be developed independently, with an addition of a belt which will wrap around them. Next, a driving angular dimension will be utilized to test the movement of the pulleys. Then, when the angle is changed, not only will the pulleys move, but the length of the belt will be updated as well.

CSWE Exam Preparation
Using Belt Chain

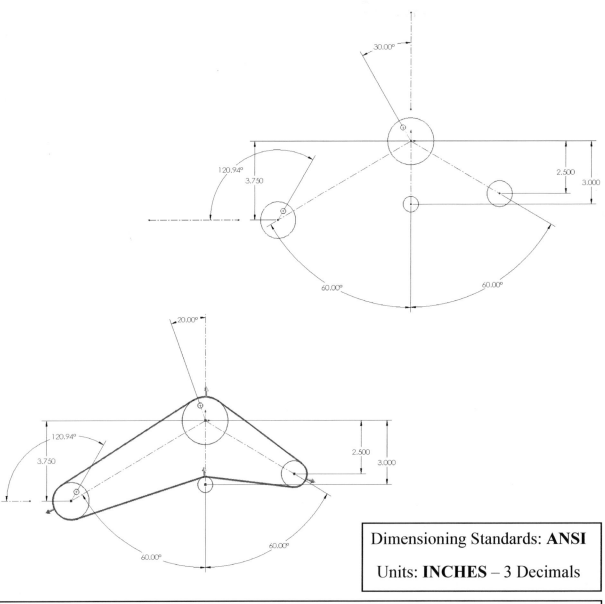

Dimensioning Standards: **ANSI**

Units: **INCHES** – 3 Decimals

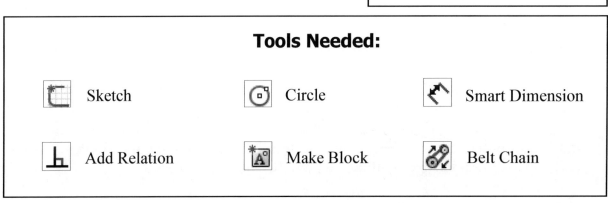

1. Starting a new part template:

- Click **File / New**.

- Select the **Part** template and click **OK**.

- Select the system of unit **IPS** from the bottom right of the screen (Inch, Pound, Second).

- Select the Front plane and open a new sketch.

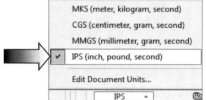

2. Creating the main sketch:

- Start sketching from the origin; add the centerlines and the circles as shown below. There should be a total of seven centerlines all together.

- There should be one vertical and one horizontal centerline that are drawn away from the rest of the entities; one of them should be coincident to the origin and the other is coincident to the center of the Ø1.750 circle. These centerlines will be used to add the driving angular and reference dimensions.

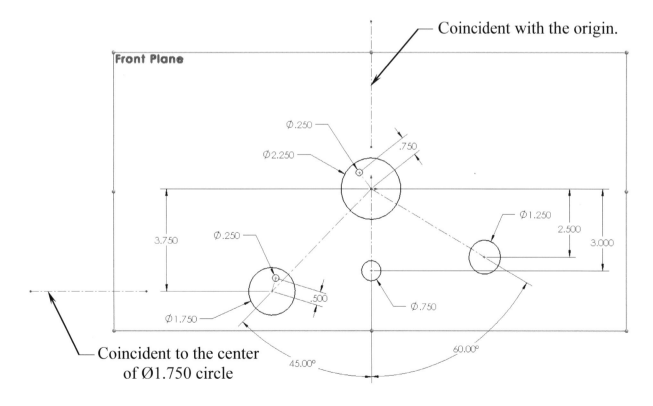

3. Making the blocks:

- A set of sketch entities and dimensions can be made into a group, or block. These blocks are used when creating the belt chain or the pulley systems.

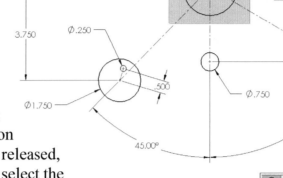

- Box-select around the upper circle, including the small circle. As soon as the mouse button is released, a small menu appears, select the **Make Block** button from it (arrow).

- We can ignore the Insertion Point since we do not need to re-use these blocks anywhere else.

- Click **OK**.

- The selected circles turn gray indicating that they have been made into a block.

- Repeat the previous step by box-selecting around the circles on the left side.

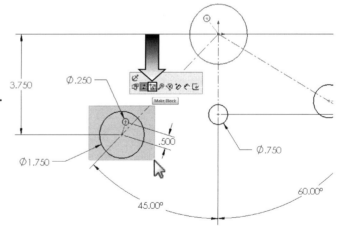

- Leave the dimensions when selecting the block, we do not need them to be part of the block.

- Click **OK**.

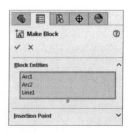

- The second block is also changed to the gray color.

1-4

- Repeat the previous step and make the third block.

- The third block has only one circle, and similar to the last steps, we can just leave out the Insertion Point.

- Click **OK**.

- The last block, block number 4, is also created the same way. This block has only the Ø1.250 circle in it.

- On the FeatureManager, there should be only one sketch with four blocks under it.

4. Creating a Belt Chain:

- Click **Tools / Sketch Entities / Belt Chain**.

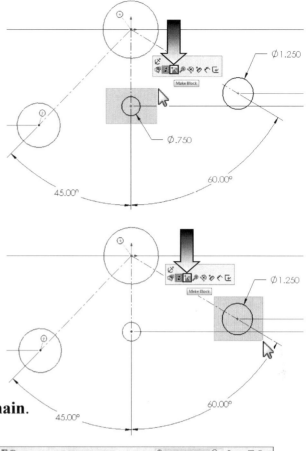

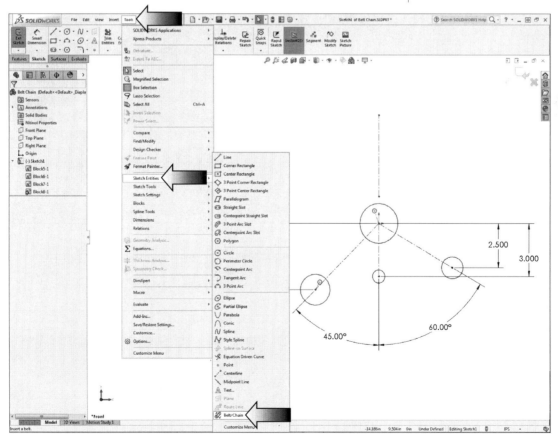

- To create a belt that wraps around these blocks, begin by clicking the circles in the order shown on the right.

- As you select the circles, the preview of a belt appears along with a "Flip Direction" arrow. Click these arrows as needed to change the wrap directions (arrow).

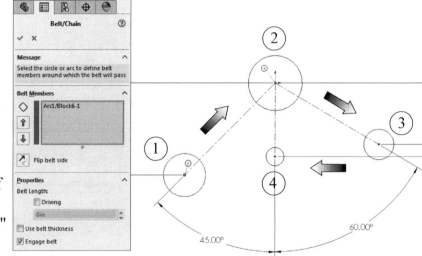

- After completing one revolution, compare your result with the image below and make any adjustments as needed. Flip the direction arrow for the small pulley as indicated.

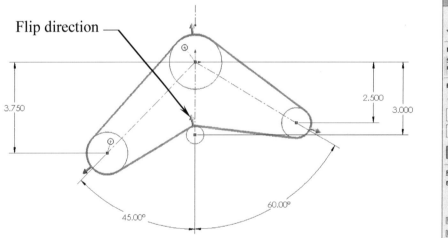

- Leave the checkbox for Driving <u>unchecked</u>. We will add a couple of Angular dimensions and use them to change the length of the belt in the next couple of steps.

- Check the length of the belt as this will be one of the questions in the Expert's exam.

- Using only two decimals, <u>enter the length</u> of your belt here:

Belt Length = _____

5. Adding the Angular dimensions:

- We are going to add a couple of angular dimensions. One of them will be used as the driving dimension, and the other, the reference dimension.

- Select the Smart-Dimension command and click the two centerlines as noted.

- Enter **30deg** for the angle and click **OK**.

- Next, add another angular dimension between the 2 lines of the 2nd block as noted. This dimension causes the sketch to become over defined, and the 1st angular dimension also turns to yellow. This indicates the two dimensions are conflicting with one another.

- Click the option: **Leave-This-Dimension-Driven** (default) to overcome the error. This option will also revert the 1st angular dimension back to its driving status.

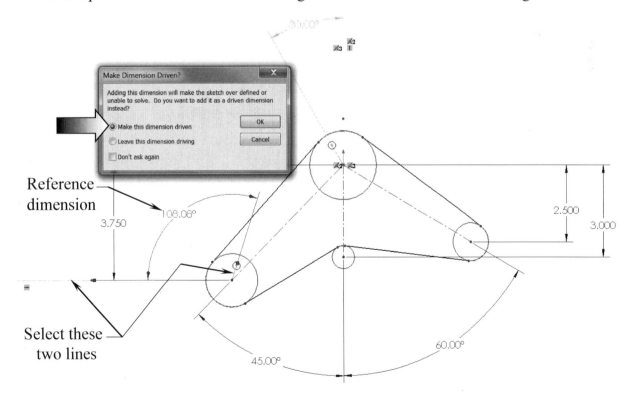

1-7

6. Applying dimension changes:

- Double click the driving dimension and change the value to **45deg**.

- Click **Rebuild** to execute the change.

- Using 2 decimals, <u>enter the value</u> of the reference dimension here: _____ deg.

- Once again, change the value of the Driving dimension from 45deg to **20deg**.

- Click **Rebuild** to update the change.

- Again, using 2 decimals enter the new value of the reference dimension here: _____ deg.

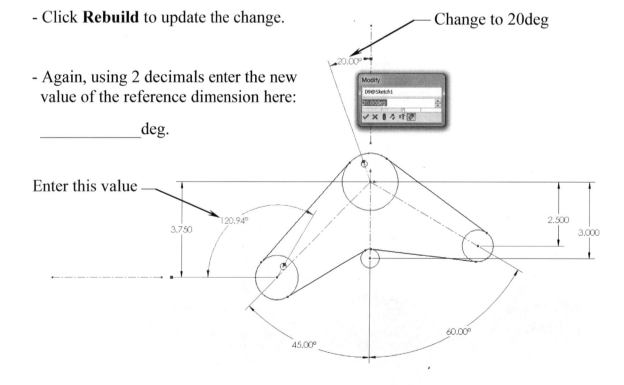

7. Checking the belt length:

- Double click the belt as noted.

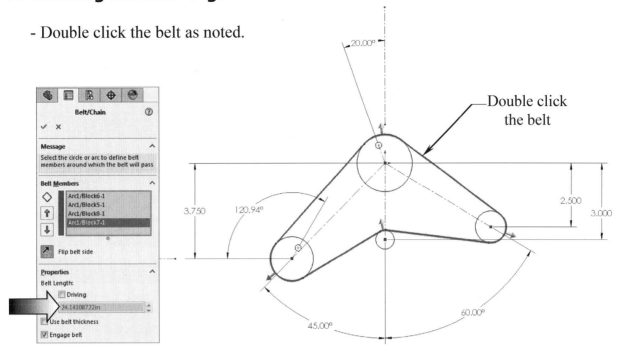

- At 20deg angle, the current belt length should be listed as **24.141in**.

- Click **OK**.

8. Changing the pulley's angle:

- Double click the 45deg dimension at the lower left corner of the sketch and change it to **60deg**.

- Click **Rebuild** to update the change.

9. Verifying the new belt length:

- Double click the belt to reactivate it.

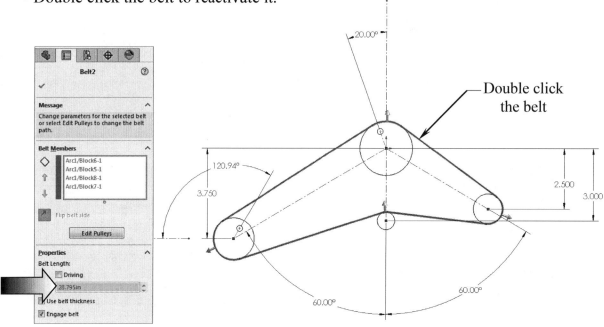

- The belt length has been increased as the result of the last dimension change.

- Enter the new belt length here: _____ in.

10. Saving your work:

- Click **File / Save As**.

- Enter **Belt Chain** for the name of the file.

- Click **Save**.

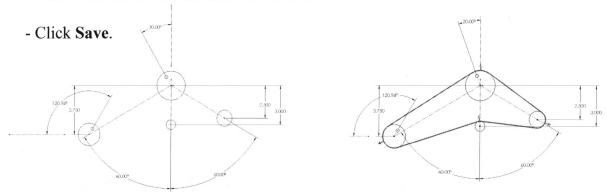

NOTE: Refer to the completed Belt Chain saved in the Training Files folder for reference, or to compare your results against it.

Exercise: Creating a Belt Chain

1. Creating the main sketch:

- Select the <u>Front</u> plane and open a new sketch.

- Sketch three circles approximately as shown and add dimensions to fully define the sketch.

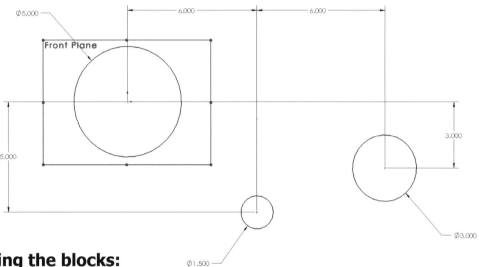

2. Making the blocks:

- Box-select the first circle on the left and click **Make Block** from the pop-up menu (arrow).

- The Make Block dialog appears on the left.

- Click **OK**.

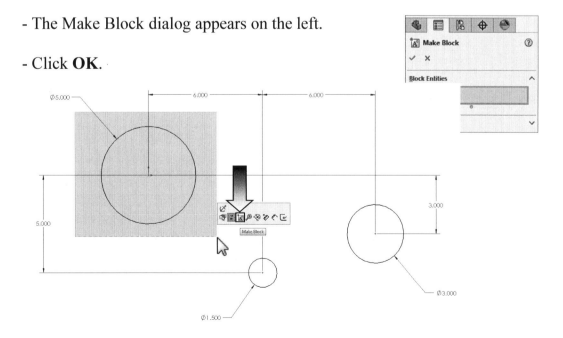

1-11

- Box-select the small circle in the middle and click the **Make Block** command once again.

- For this exercise, we will not need to create the Insertion Points for any of the blocks, since they will not need to be scaled or saved separately.

- Click **OK**.

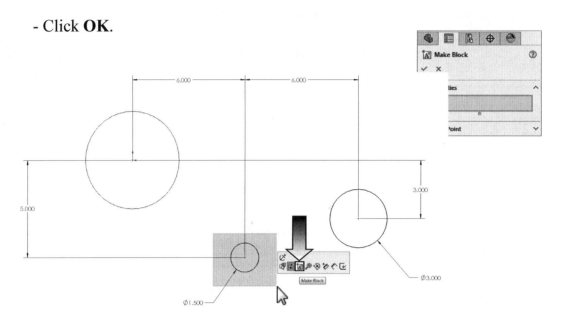

- Repeat the same step and make the third block from the last circle.

NOTE: When making the blocks there is no order for which block you should make first or last; however when creating a Belt Chain you may have to follow a certain order to define the direction of the belt.

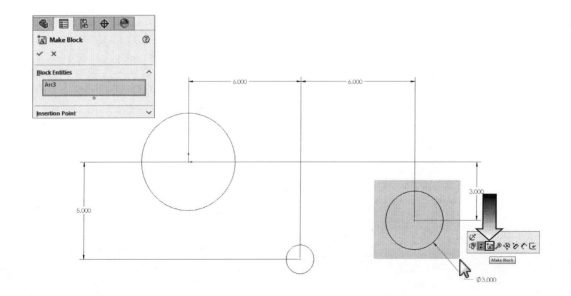

3. Creating the Belt Chain:

- From the Tools drop down menu, select: **Sketch Entities / Belt Chain**.

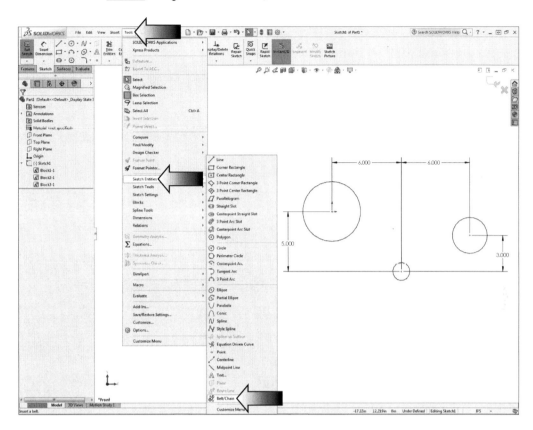

- Start the belt by clicking the largest circle on the left, then the smallest circle in the middle, and finally, the one on the right.

- The preview of a belt appears along with the belt length.

- The current length of the belt is about **38.140in** (3 decimals).

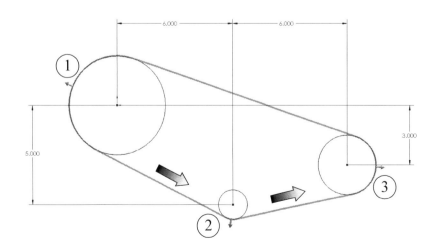

- Click **OK**.

- We are going to remove the 3.000 vertical dimension for now and later replace it with an angular dimension.

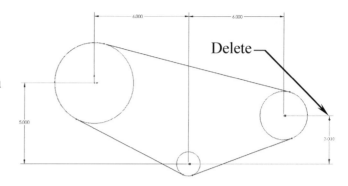

- The two lines on the right change to the blue color which indicates an under defined status.

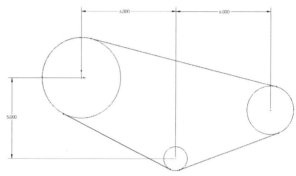

- <u>Drag</u> the center point of the largest circle away from the origin.

Drag the center to move it away from the origin

- Add a **Coincident** relation between the center of the large circle and the origin.

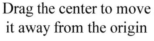

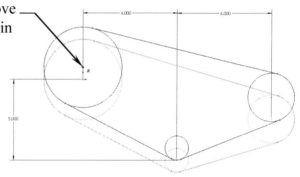

Add a Coincident relation

- Click **Rebuild** to update the sketch.

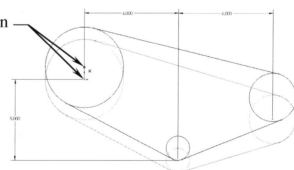

- <u>**Edit**</u> the Sketch1 from the FeatureManager tree.

- There should be three blocks tied to the Sketch1.

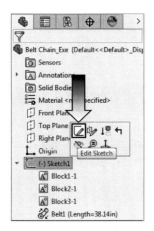
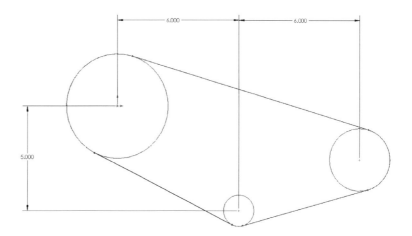

4. Adding an angular dimension:

- Select the **Smart Dimension** command and click the centers of the three circles in the order as labeled 1, 2, and 3 (clockwise direction).

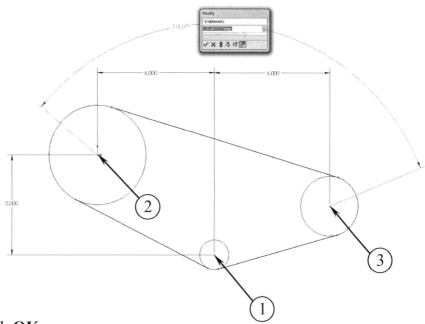

- Click **OK**.

- The default angle is about **115° to 122°**, we will change it in the next step.

- This angle also determines the length of the belt. Changing this angular dimension will also change the belt length.

5. Changing the angular dimension:

- Double click the Angular dimension and change its value to **135.00°**.

- Press the **Rebuild** button on the Modify box to execute the change.

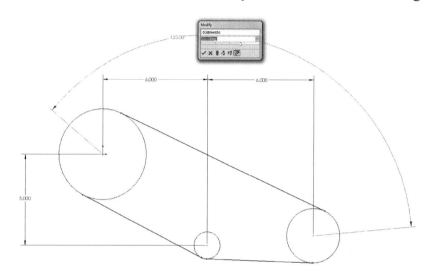

6. Verifying the belt length:

- **Edit** the Sketch1 from the Feature tree and double click the belt to edit it.

- The dimension change has updated the belt length to **38.556in**.

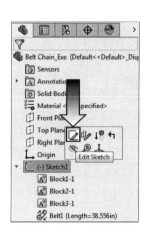

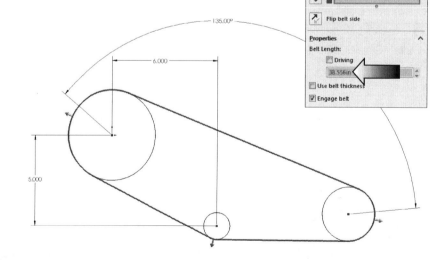

- Click **OK**.

7. Saving your work:

- Save your work as **Belt Chain_Exe**.

- Close all documents.

CHAPTER 2

Advanced Weldments

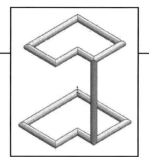

CSWE Exam Preparation
Advanced Weldments

This chapter discusses the details of the Advanced-Weldments challenge in the new CSWE examination.

You will be asked to create the weldment part and make use of the weldment functionality such as:

* 3D Sketch

* Advanced weldment part creation

* Locating and applying the structural member

* Trim/Extend Command

* Weldment corner modification

* Weldment Part modification

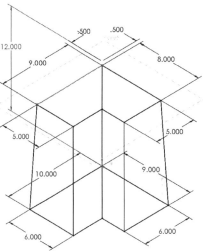

The Corner Treatments command offers several options, but only one type hidden well inside the Trim Order will provide the right solution to the challenge.

After the right corners are applied, you will need to calculate the mass as the answer to the question.

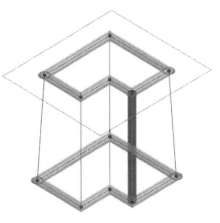

CSWE 2017 | Exam Preparation | Advanced Weldments

CSWE Exam Preparation
Advanced Weldments

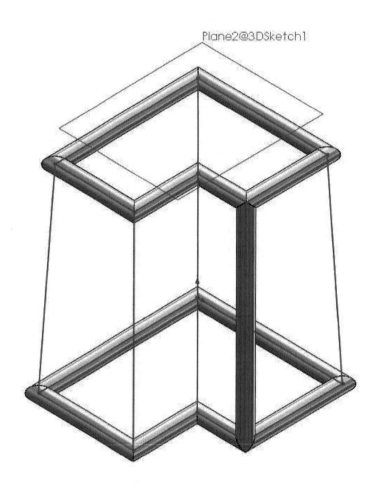

Dimensioning Standards: **ANSI**

Units: **INCHES** – 3 Decimals

Tools Needed:

3D Sketch	Line	Weldment Feature
Structural Member	Trim Extend	Mass Properties

1. Starting a new Part template:

- Select **File / New / Part**.

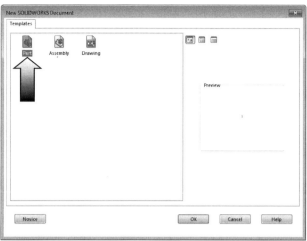

- The Advanced Weldments Frame will be built from scratch to test your skills on the use of the weldments functionalities such as Structural Members, Weldment Profiles, Trimming / Extending the weldment groups, and on top of all that, creating and constraining 3D sketches.

2. Creating a 3D Sketch:

- Select **3D Sketch** from the sketch drop down arrow.

- Select the **Line** command and sketch the first line along the **X direction**.

NOTE: Keep the cursor on the dotted line to make a straight line. Pay attention to the yellow icon and its Along X direction (or Along Y, Along Z).

- Sketch the second line along the **Z direction**. Press the **TAB** key to change direction when needed.

- The tab key flips the direction by **90 degrees**, changing from X to Z, and then to Y direction simultaneously.

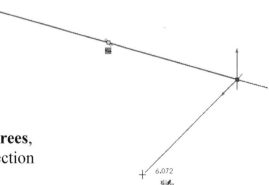

2-3

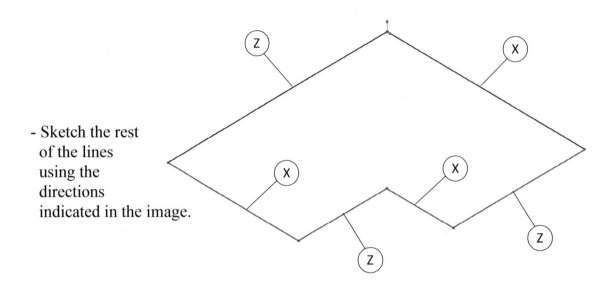

- Sketch the rest of the lines using the directions indicated in the image.

- Add the dimensions shown below to fully define the first portion of the sketch.

NOTE: *It is easier and more proper to dimension "from a line to a line" to keep the dimension parallel to the line (see note below).*

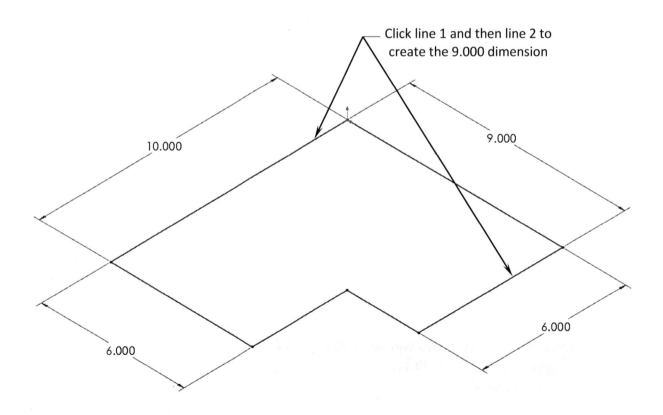

- Remain in the 3D Sketch mode.

- The second portion of the sketch will be drawn on a new plane but within the same sketch.

- Click the **Plane** command (arrow).

- For the First Reference, select the **Top** plane (arrow).

- For the Second Reference, click the **Distance** button and enter **12.00in** (arrow).

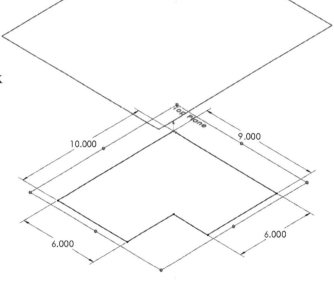

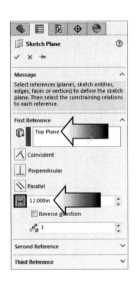

- Place the new plane <u>above</u> the Top plane.

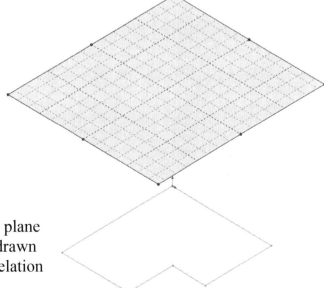

- The grids on the plane mean the plane is active; sketch entities can be drawn on this plane, and an On Plane relation will be added to each entity.

3. Creating the second portion of the 3D Sketch:

- Ensure that the new plane is still active (double clicking on the plane will activate or de-activate it).

- Sketch the additional lines as shown on the right.

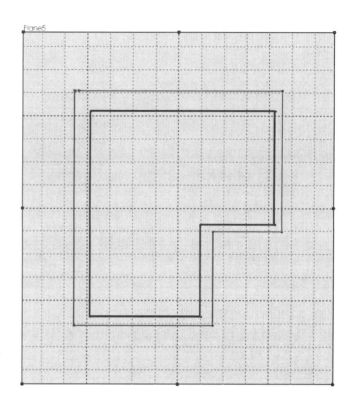

NOTE: *When sketching on a plane, the relations will change back to Vertical and Horizontal instead of Along X and Along Y.*

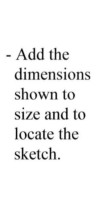

- Add the dimensions shown to size and to locate the sketch.

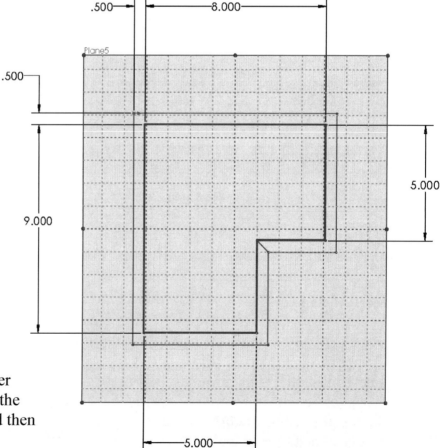

- The sketch should still be under defined at this point. We will add other lines to connect the two portions and then fully define it.

2-6

- Double click outside the plane to **deactivate** it. The grids on the plane should disappear.

- Change to the **Isometric** orientation (Control+7).

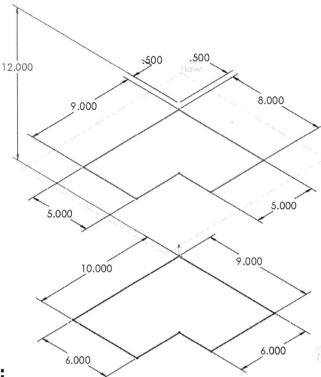

- Your sketch should look similar to the one shown on the right.

4. Connecting the sketch entities:

- Remain in the same 3D sketch.

- Select the **Line** command and sketch a line that connects the lower with the upper portion.

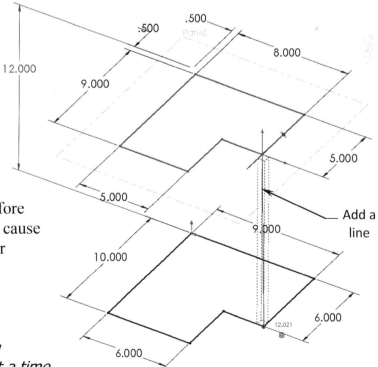

- Avoid adding the Along-Z relation by rotating the view slightly to a side before adding the line, as it may cause the sketch to become over defined when adding the dimensions in the next couple steps.

NOTE: Use the Click+Hold+Drag technique to add 1 line at a time.

- Continue with adding the lines as shown in the image on the right.

- Add an **Along Z** relation to the line on top-left as noted.

- The sketch should be fully defined at this point.

- **Exit** the 3D Sketch or press Control+Q.

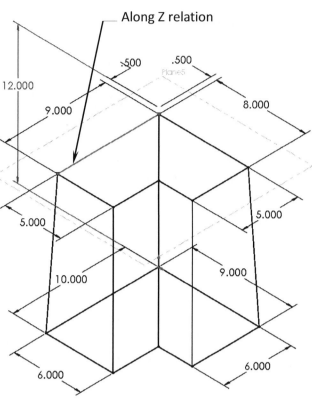

5. Adding the structural members:

- Change to the **Weldments** tab. (Right click the Evaluate tab and enable the Weldments tab if needed.)

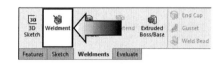

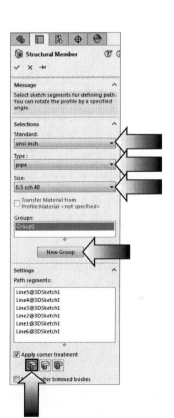

- Click the **Structural Member** button (arrow).

- For Standard, select **Ansi Inch**.

- For Type, select **Pipe**.

- For Size, select **0.5 sch 40**.

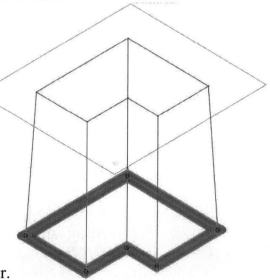

- Click the **New Group** button and select the 6 lines at the bottom. Keep the Corner-Treatment at End Miter.

2-8

- A group is a collection of related segments in a structural member.

- To create a group, select a series of segments on the sketch. The second segment you select determines the type of group you are creating.

- Click the **New-Group** button and select the 6 lines on top of the sketch.

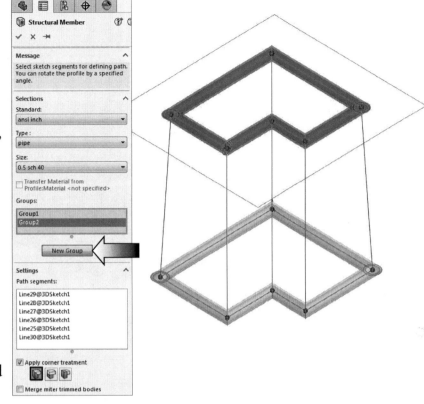

- Keep all other parameters the same as the last group.

- Click **OK** to exit the Structural Member command.

6. Assigning the material:

- Although different materials can be assigned to each weldment body individually, for this exercise we will assign the same material to all weldment bodies.

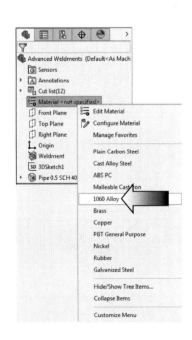

- Right click the **Material** option on the Feature tree and select **1060 Alloy** (arrow).
  Mass Property for the entire weldment part can now be calculated.

7. Calculating the Mass:

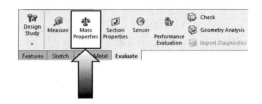

- Switch to the **Evaluate** tab.

- Click the **Mass Properties** command (arrow).

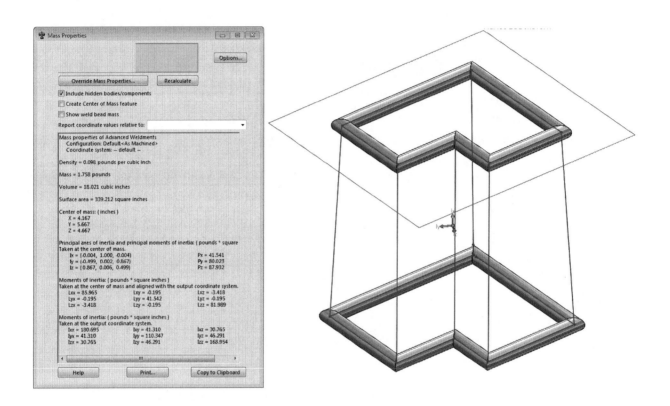

- Locate the mass of the weldment part and enter it here: _____ pounds.

(Keep the part open for the next step).

8. Adding more groups:

- Locate the feature **Pipe 0.5 SCH 40** from the Feature tree, right click it and select **Edit Feature** (arrow).

- Click the **New Group** button (arrow) to add a new group to the existing weldment part.

- Keep all parameters at their default values.

- Select the **line** as noted to add the same structural member to it.

- The 2 corners of the new tube must be modified.

- Select the **bottom corner** as indicated to bring out the Corner Treatment dialog box.

- Change the **Trim Order** to **2** (arrow). This option reverses the corners to the correct type.

- Click **OK**.

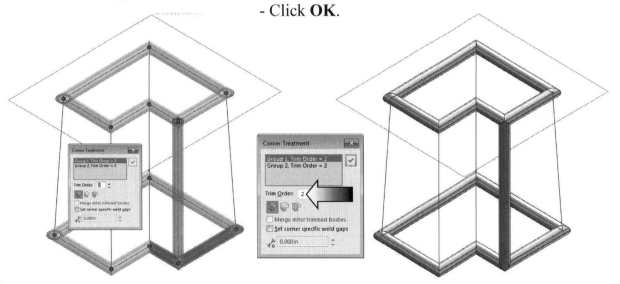

2-11

9. Calculating the Mass:

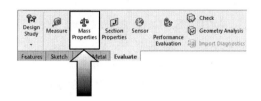

- Switch to the **Evaluate** tab.

- Click the **Mass Properties** command (arrow).

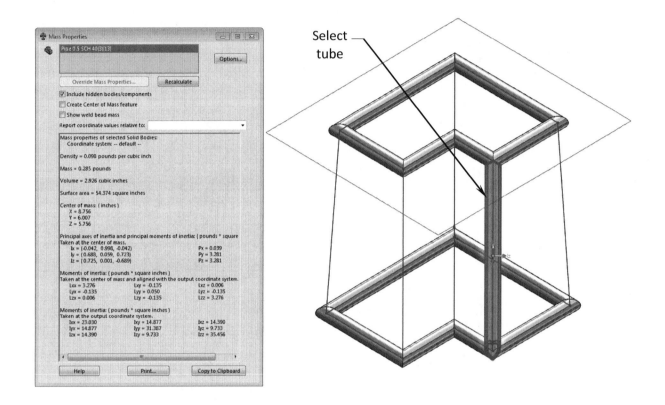

- Locate the mass of the new structural member and enter it here: _____ lbs.

(Keep the part open for the next step).

10. Modifying the dimensions:

- Select the 3D Sketch from the Feature tree to display all of its dimensions.

- Locate the overall height dimension **12.000** (circled) and change it to **10.000in**.

- Change the length dimension on the top left (circled) from **9.000** to **7.000in**.

- Change the length dimension on the top right (circled) from **5.000** to **4.000in**.

- Press the **Rebuild** 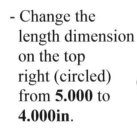 button to execute the dimension changes.

- The weldment part should look like the one shown on the right.

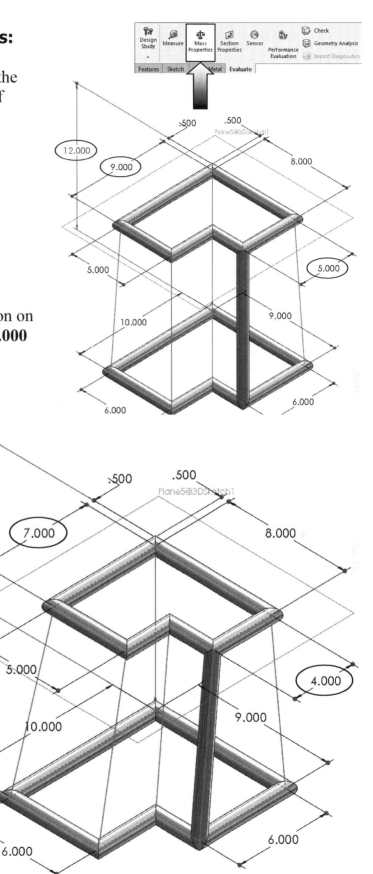

11. Calculating the Mass:

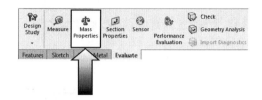

- Switch to the **Evaluate** tab.

- Click the **Mass Properties** command (arrow).

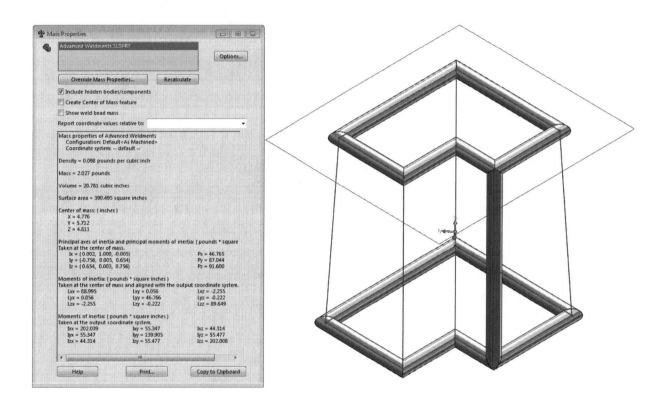

- Locate the mass of the weldment part and enter it here: _____ pounds.

12. Saving your work:

- Select File / Save As.

- Enter: **Advanced Weldment.sldprt** for the name of the part.

- Click **Save**.

CHAPTER 3

Advanced Sheet Metal

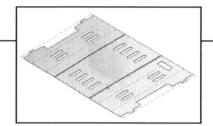

CSWE Exam Preparation
Advanced Sheet Metal

This chapter discusses a method of importing an IGES document and converting it into a SOLIDWORKS sheet metal part.

In order for the conversion to work properly, the imported part must have a constant thickness. During the conversion, the Convert to Sheet Metal PropertyManager is used to assist you to specify sheet metal parameters such as: the fixed face, the thickness of the sheet metal part, the default bend radius, and the edges or fillet faces on which to create bends. If an edge already has a fillet applied, the radius of the fillet is used as the bend radius for the new sheet metal part.

SOLIDWORKS automatically selects the edges on which rips are applied. However, you can also manually select rip edges using rip sketches.

When using the Convert to Sheet Metal tool, you can keep the solid body to use with multiple Convert to Sheet Metal features.

After the imported part is converted to a SOLIDWOKS sheet metal part you can flatten it to measure the overall bounding box of the sheet, or unfolding it to add other cut features in the flat mode, and then return the bends to their folded stage along with the cut features.

The overall length and mass of the part will be used as the answers to each question.

CSWE Exam Preparation
Advanced Sheet Metal

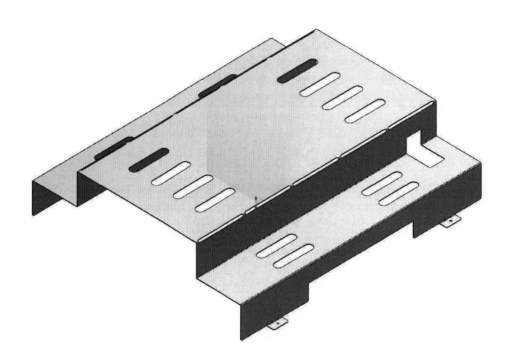

Dimensioning Standards: **ANSI**

Units: **INCHES** – 3 Decimals

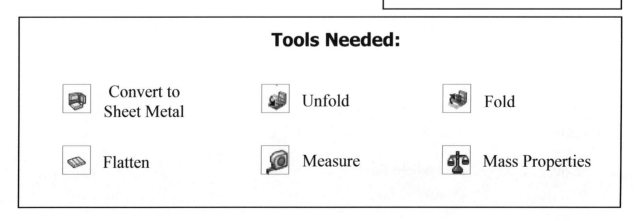

1. Opening an IGES document:

- Select **File / Open**.

- Change the File Type to IGES.

- Browse to the Training Files folder and select the document named:
Advanced Sheet Metal.IGS

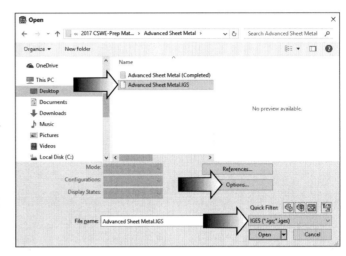

- Click the **Option** button.

- Enable/disable the options shown in the dialog box on the right.

- Click **OK** and click **Open**.

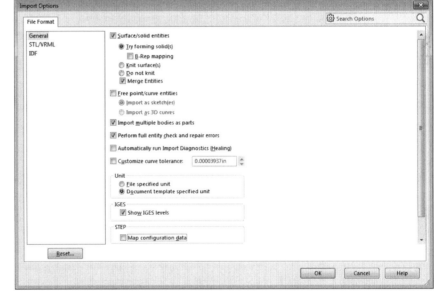

- The IGES-In dialog appears, select/unselect the options shown.

- Click **OK** to close the IGES-In dialog box.

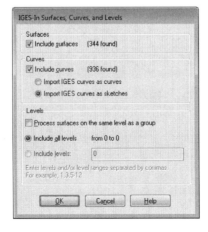

- Click **OK** again to accept and close the Import Free Points and Curves dialog box.

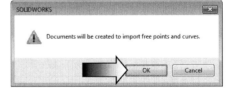

- The IGES file is imported into a SOLIDWORKS part document template.

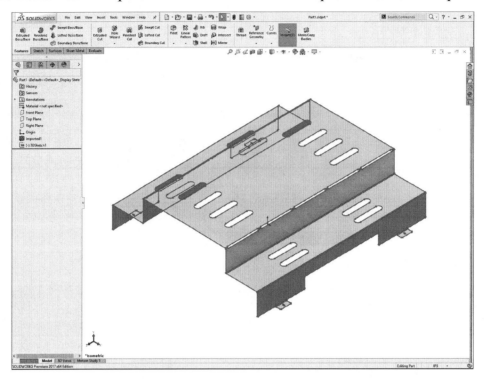

2. Changing the Display Style:

- It is much easier to work with a model when its edges are visible in the shaded mode.

- Locate the Heads-Up View toolbar, expand the Display-Style and select: **Shaded With Edges** (arrow).

- The edges of the imported model are now visible.

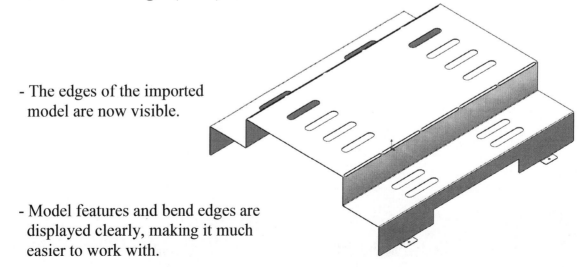

- Model features and bend edges are displayed clearly, making it much easier to work with.

3. Enabling the Sheet Metal tool tab:

- It is also quicker to use the icons on the tool tabs than using the drop down menus.

- Right click one of the tabs (Features, Sketch, or Evaluate, etc.) and enable the **Sheet Metal** tools.

4. Converting to sheet metal:

- Change to the Sheet Metal tab.

- Click the **Convert to Sheet Metal** command.

- For Fixed Face, select the top face of the model as noted.

- For thickness, enter **.059in**.

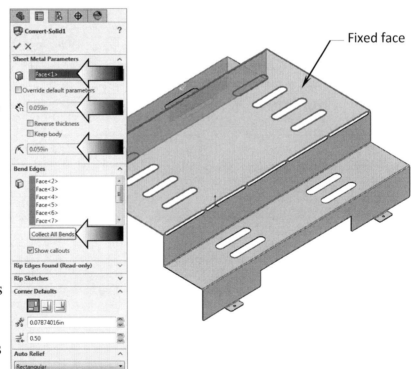

- For Bend Edges, click **Collect All Bend**s.

- For Corner Defaults select **Open Butt**. Set the **Gap** to **.0787**, and Overlaps to **.50**.

- Keep Auto Relief at the default **Rectangular** type, and click **OK**.

5. Measuring the flat length:

- Click the **Flatten** command on the Sheet Metal tab.

- Change to the **Evaluate** tab.

- Click the **Measure** command.

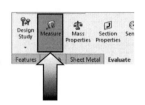

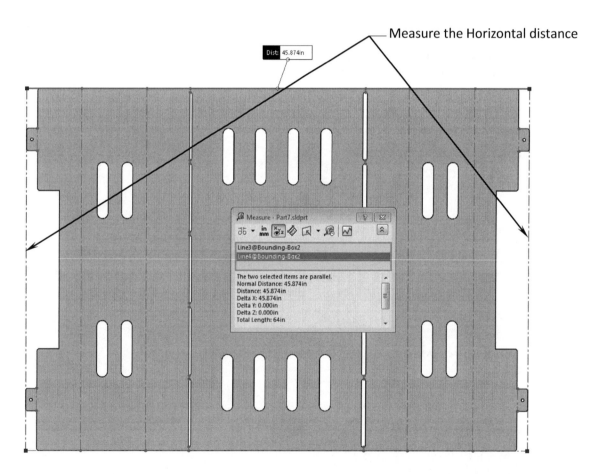

- Measure the Normal Distance (the longest horizontal distance) of the flat pattern and enter it here: _____ in.

6. Unfolding the bends:

- With the Unfold and Fold tools, you can flatten one more bends in a sheet metal part. This combination is useful when adding a cut across a bend. First, add an Unfold feature to flatten the bend. Next, add your cut. Lastly, add a Fold feature to return the bend to its folded state.

- Select the **Unfold** command (arrow).

- For Fixed Face, select the upper face as indicated.

- Click **Collect All Bends**.

- Click **OK**.

- Select the face indicated and open a new sketch.

- Sketch a **rectangle** and add the dimensions shown.

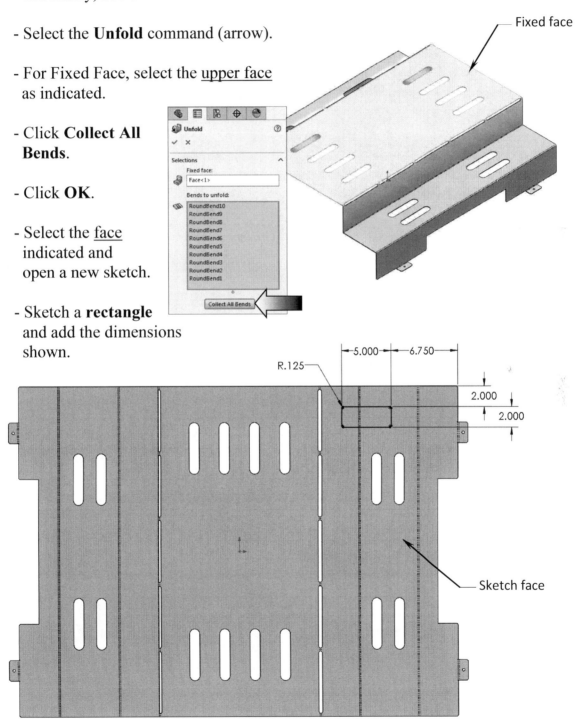

3-7

7. Extruding a cut:

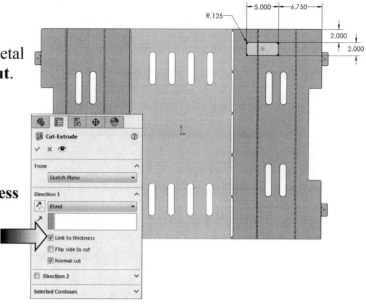

- Switch back to the Sheet Metal tab and press: **Extruded Cut**.

- Use the default **Blind** type.

- Enable the **Link to Thickness** checkbox.

- Click **OK**.

8. Folding the bends:

- Click the **Fold** command.

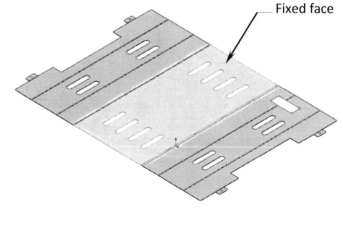

- The Fixed Face should be selected already.

- Click **Collect All Bends**.

- Click **OK**. The bends are returned to their folded stage, along with the cut feature.

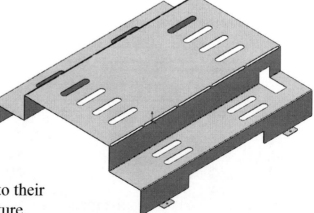

9. Assigning material:

- Physical (or mechanical) properties of the material must be assigned to the model in order to calculate its mass properties.

- Right click the Material option on the Feature tree and select **1060 Alloy** (arrow).

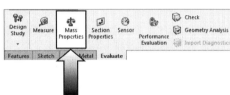

10. Calculating the mass:

- Change to the **Evaluate** tab.

- Click **Mass Properties**.

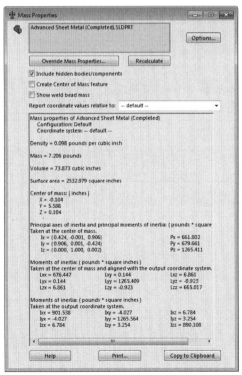

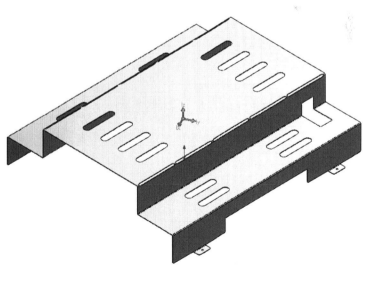

- Locate the Mass of the model and enter it here: _____ pounds.

11. Saving your work:

- Select **File / Save As**.

- Enter: **Advanced Sheet Metal.sldprt** for the file name.

- Click **Save**.

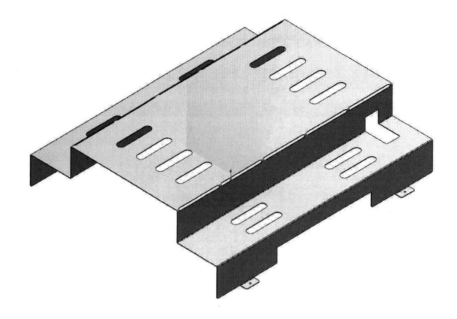

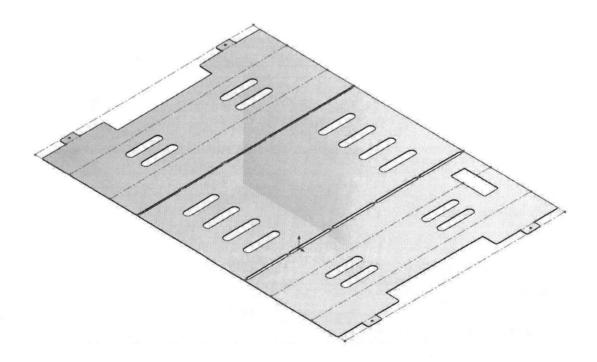

CHAPTER 4

Cam Motions

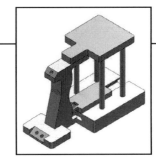

CSWE Exam Preparation
Cam Motions

This chapter will discuss the use of Tangent mate vs. the Cam Follower mate.

A cam-follower mate is like a tangent and a coincident mate combined. It allows you to mate a cylinder, plane, or point to a series of tangent extruded faces, such as you would find on a cam.

The cam part must form a closed loop and the follower can be a vertex, a planar or non-planar face.

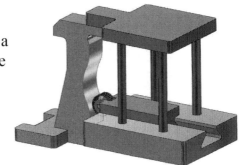

A Tangent mate is a little more "flexible" than a Cam mate. Almost any type of geometry can be used to create a tangent mate such as a line, a cone, a solid or surface body, a cylinder or a sphere, etc., and the geometry can either be open or closed.

In this chapter, the component Wheel has teeth which make it a little difficult to select. Therefore a cylindrical surface was created around the teeth to help mating it to the Cam part more easily. The Cam mate cannot be used in this case because the cam path does not form a closed loop. We will use a Tangent mate to constraint the Wheel to the Cam part and still get the same result.

After creating the Tangent mate, you will be asked to measure the Minimum and Maximum distances between the components, and enter them as the answer to each question.

CSWE 2017 | Exam Preparation | Cam Motions

CSWE Exam Preparation
Cam Motions

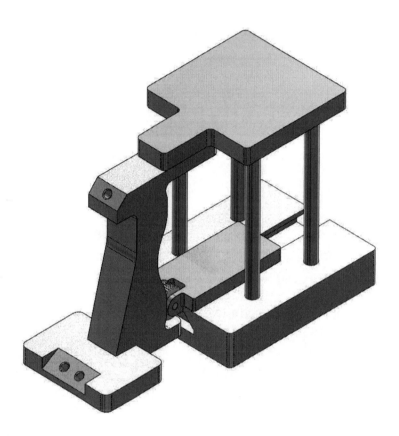

Dimensioning Standards: **ANSI**

Units: **INCHES** – 3 Decimals

Tools Needed:

 Assembly Document   Mate

 Tangent Mate   Measure

1. Opening an assembly document:

- Select **File / Open**.

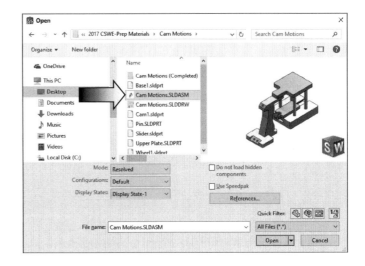

- Browse to the Training Files folder and open the assembly document named: **Cam Motions.sldasm**

- The assembly has been partially constrained. Some of the components still have one or more degrees of freedom, which allow them to move or rotate about the open directions.

- One quick way to see which component is still under defined is to look for the minus sign (-) in front of their names.

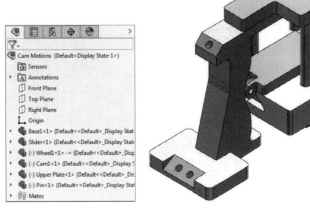

- The component that does not have the minus sign in front of its name means it is fully defined, it can no longer be moved or rotated. Only the Base and the Slider are fully mated, the others are still under defined.

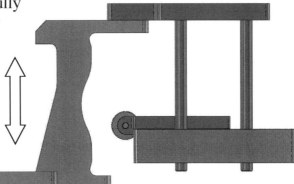

- Check the existing constraints by dragging the Cam-part up and down, also left and right.
Only the Upper Plate should move with the Cam part.

2. Adding a Tangent mate:

- Since the faces in the Cam part do not form a closed loop, a tangent mate will need to be used here to constraint the Wheel to the Cam part.

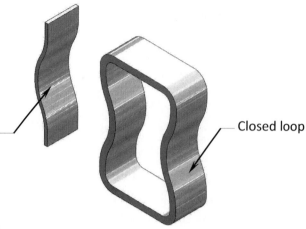

- Switch to the Assembly tool tab and select the **Mate** command.

- Select the curved face of the Cam part and the cylindrical face of the of the Wheel.

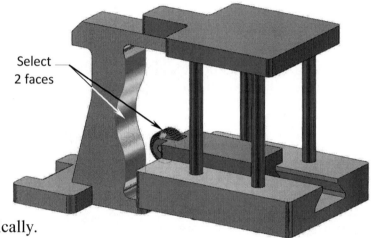

- The **Tangent** mate option is selected automatically.

- Click **OK** to accept the mate.

- **Exit** the mate mode.

- Drag the Cam part up and down to verify the new Tangent mate. The Slider, the Wheel, and the Upper Plate should move along with the Cam part.

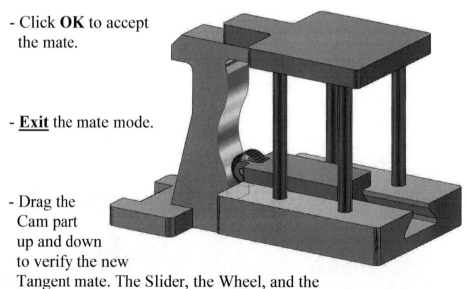

3. Measuring the Minimum Distance:

- Drag the Cam part <u>downward</u> and also to the right.

- The Cam part should stop when it reaches the end of the cam path, and the Wheel should barely touch the Cam part at the top.

- Switch to the **Evaluate** tab.

- Measure the distance between the upper face of the Base and the under face of the Upper-Plate.

- Enter the minimum distance here:

_____

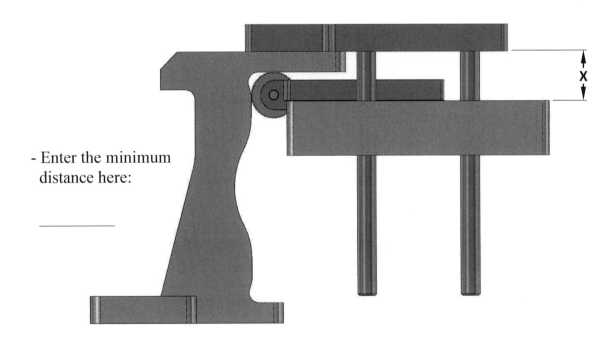

4. Measuring the Maximum Distance:

- Drag the Cam part <u>upward</u> and all the way to the right.

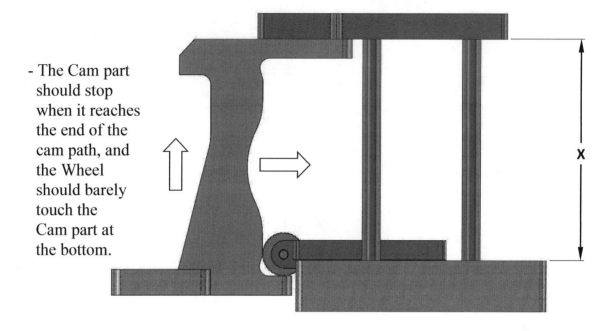

- The Cam part should stop when it reaches the end of the cam path, and the Wheel should barely touch the Cam part at the bottom.

- Measure the distance between the same two faces (the upper face of the Base and the under face of the Upper-Plate).

- Enter the maximum distance here: _____

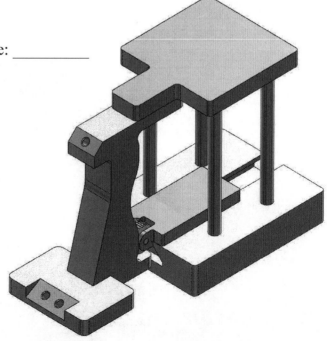

5. Saving your work:

- Select **File / Save As**.

- Enter Cam **Motions.sldasm** for the file name.

- Press **Save**.

- Close all documents.

CHAPTER 5

Assembly Drawings & BOM

CSWE Exam Preparation
Assembly Drawings & BOM

This chapter will guide you through the creation of an assembly drawing.

Only an Isometric drawing view will be needed for this chapter.
Using the Isometric drawing view as the reference, a Bill of Materials is inserted and modified to include:

* Top level
* Parts-only
* Indented
* Part configuration grouping
* Accessing custom properties in BOM
* Item numbers and their display

ITEM NO.	PART NUMBER	DESCRIPTION	QTY.
1	Stand		1
2	Grate		2
3	Grill Base		1
4	Handle		3
5	Grill Lid		1
6	Cooking Grid		1
7	Pin		1

ITEM NO.	PART NUMBER	DESCRIPTION	SW-Configuration Name(Configuration Name)	QTY.	SW-File Name(File Name)
1	Stand		42-Inches	1	Stand
2	Grate		10 Degrees	2	Grate
3	Grill Base		Default	1	Grill Base
4	Handle		Wood	3	Handle
5	Grill Lid		Default	1	Grill Lid
6	Cooking Grid		Default	1	Cooking Grid
7	Pin		Default	1	Pin

You will be asked to create the Custom Properties to show the configurations of the components as well as the sub-assemblies in the BOM. The answer to each question will be one of the results displayed by each custom property you created.

This section earns 40 points total in the CSWE exam.

CSWE 2017 | Exam Preparation | Assembly Drawings & BOM

CSWE Exam Preparation
Assembly Drawings & BOM

ITEM NO.	PART NUMBER	DESCRIPTION	SW-Configuration Name(Configuration Name)	QTY.	Finish
1	Stand Sub		10 Degrees	1	
	Stand		42-Inches	1	
	Grate		10 Degrees	2	
2	Grill Base Sub		Wood Handle	1	
	Grill Base		Default	1	Black Annodized
	Handle		Wood	2	
3	Grill Lid Sub		Wood Handle	1	
	Grill Lid		Default	1	
	Handle		Wood	1	
4	Cooking Grid		Default	1	
5	Pin		Default	1	

Dimensioning Standards: **ANSI**

Units: **INCHES** – 3 Decimals

Tools Needed:

- Drawing Template
- Bill of Materials
- View Palette
- Sub-Assembly

Column type: **CUSTOM PROPERTY**
Property name: **SW-File Name(File Name)**

1. Opening an assembly document:

- Select **File / Open**.

- Browse to the Training Files folder and open the assembly document named:
Grill Assembly.sldasm

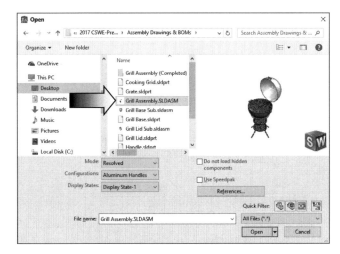

- This assembly document has four sub-assemblies, two components, and two assembly configurations.

- Some of the components also have their own configurations previously created. (Open the part files to see them listed on the ConfigurationManager.)

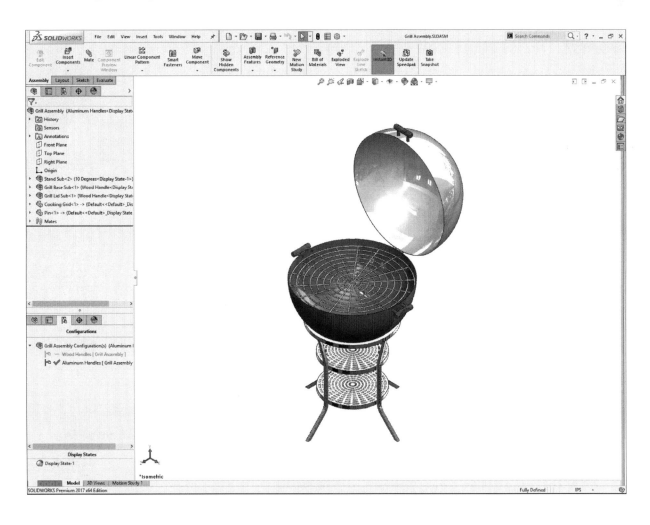

2. Transferring to a drawing:

- We will transfer the assembly to a drawing so that a Bill of Materials and Custom Properties can be added to display the configurations and/or the quantity of the components.

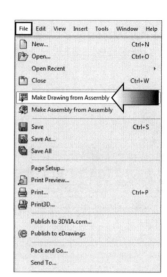

- Select **File / Make Drawing from Assembly** (arrow).

- Select the **Drawing** template (arrow).

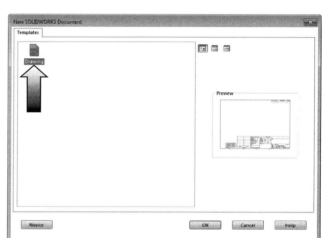

- A default drawing template is loaded. Right click inside the drawing and select **Properties**.

- Set the following:

    * **Scale: 1:16**

    * **Third Angle Projection**

    * **B (ANSI) Landscape**

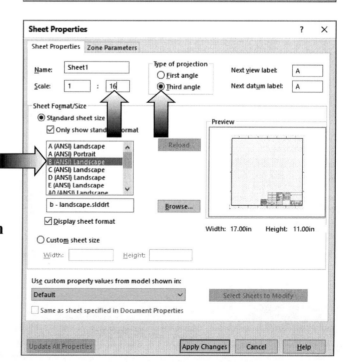

- Click **Apply Changes**.

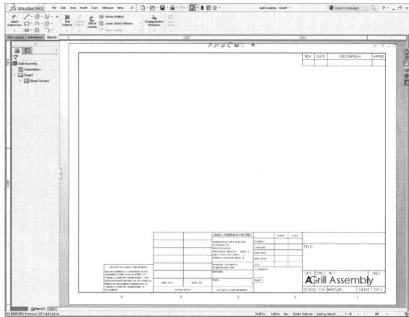

- The B size drawing template is loaded. (The Title Block does not need to be filled out for this exercise.)

3. Adding an Isometric Drawing view:

- Expand the **View Palette** (arrow).

- Drag and drop the isometric drawing view into the drawing, approximately as shown.

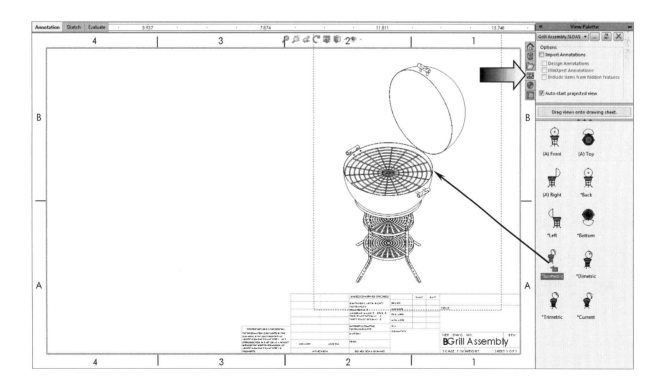

4. Adding a Bill of Materials:

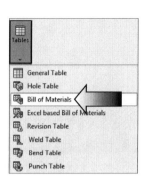

- This section will examine your skills on customizing the Bill of Materials such as adding new columns, displaying the existing configurations, and creating custom properties.

- Click the Isometric drawing view's border and select: **Tables / Bill of materials** from the Annotation tab (arrow).

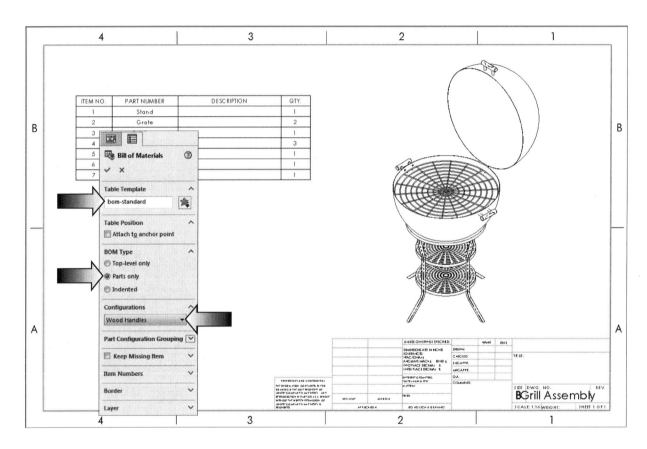

- Use the default **BOM Standard** template and set the BOM Type to **Parts Only**.

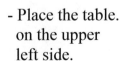

- Select **Wood Handles** for Configurations

- Place the table on the upper left side.

- Right click the **Column C** and select: **Insert / Column Right**.

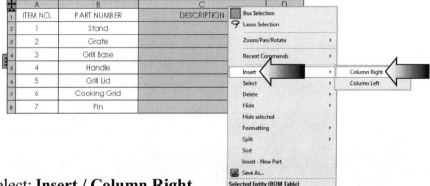

5-6

5. Changing the Column Property:

- In the pop-up box, select **Custom Property** under Column Type (arrow).

- For Property Name, select **SW-Configuration Name** (arrow).

6. Locating the quantity:

- Locate the Part Number **Wood** and the SW-Configuration **Handle**

- Enter the **QTY** of the Wood Handle: _____

7. Creating another Custom Property:

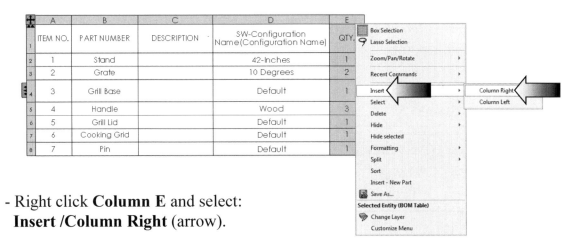

- Right click **Column E** and select:
  Insert /Column Right (arrow).

- For Column Type, select **Custom Property**.

- For Property Name, select **Finish** from the list (arrow).

	A	B	C	D	E	F
1	ITEM NO.	PART NUMBER	DESCRIPTION	SW-Configuration Name(Configuration Name)	QTY.	
2	1	Stand		42-Inches	1	
3	2	Grate		10 Degrees	2	
4	3	Grill Base		Default	1	
5	4	Handle		Wood	3	
6	5	Grill Lid		Default	1	
7	6	Cooking Grid		Default	1	
8	7	Pin		Default	1	

8. Locating the Finish:

- Locate the Part Number Grill Base (Item number 4).

- Enter the **Finish** of the Grill Base here: _____.

	A	B	C	D	E	F
1	ITEM NO.	PART NUMBER	DESCRIPTION	SW-Configuration Name(Configuration Name)	QTY.	Finish
2	1	Stand		42-Inches	1	
3	2	Grate		10 Degrees	2	
4	3	Grill Base		Default	1	Black Annodized
5	4	Handle		Wood	3	
6	5	Grill Lid		Default	1	
7	6	Cooking Grid		Default	1	
8	7	Pin		Default	1	

- The drawing should look similar to the one shown on the right at this point.

- You do not have to add the balloons.

- Next, we will change the BOM Type to show the components inside the sub-assemblies.

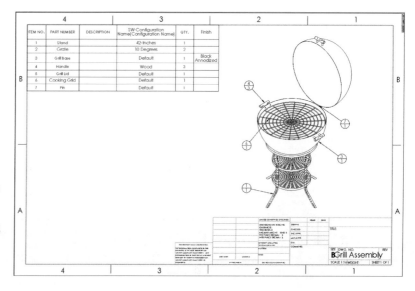

9. Changing the BOM Type:

- Click the **Pan icon** on the upper left corner of the BOM to display its settings.

- Change the BOM Type to **Indented** (arrow). This option indents subassembly components below their subassemblies.

- Select: **No numbering**.

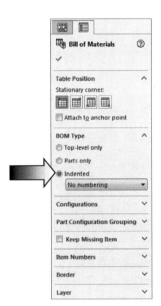

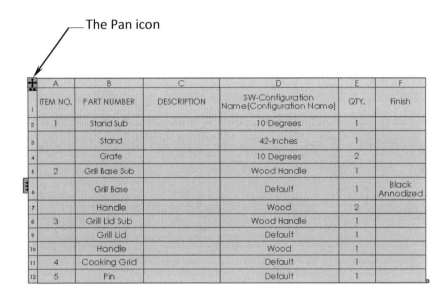

The Pan icon

10. Locating the sub-component:

- Locate the sub-component named: Grate, under the column B (arrow).

- Which sub-assembly does the component Grate belongs to?
  Check one.

☐ Stand Sub

☐ Grill Base Sub

☐ Grill Lid Sub

☐ Cooking Grid

11. Saving your work:

- Select **File / Save As**.

- Use the default name **Grill Assembly.slddrw**

- Click **Save**.

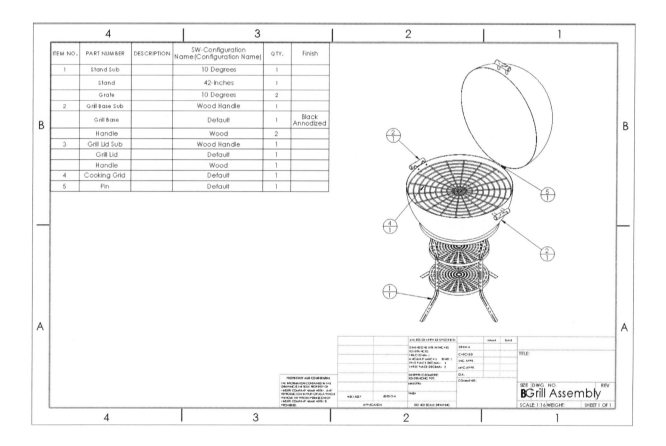

- Close all documents

CHAPTER 6

Assembly Modifications

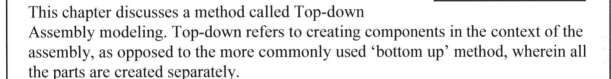

CSWE Exam Preparation
Assembly Modifications

This chapter discusses a method called Top-down Assembly modeling. Top-down refers to creating components in the context of the assembly, as opposed to the more commonly used 'bottom up' method, wherein all the parts are created separately.

In top-down assembly design, one or more features of a part are defined by one or more entities in an assembly, such as a layout sketch or the geometry of another part. The design intent such as the sizes of features, placement of components in the assembly, proximity to other parts, etc. comes from the assembly and moves down into the parts.

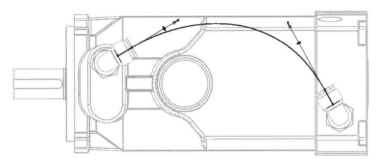

In this chapter, the locations and the diameters of the two fittings will be used to precisely create the copper pipe. Not only will this method allow you to control the clearance between the fitting and the pipe, but the time it takes to create the pipe would be far less than other assembly methods.

After the copper pipe is created, material will be assigned, and the center of mass of the assembly will be calculated as the answer to this challenge.

CSWE 2017 | Exam Preparation | Assembly Modifications

CSWE Exam Preparation
Assembly Modifications

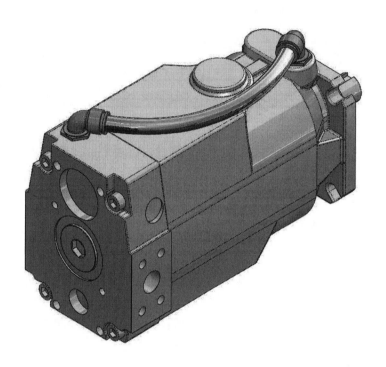

Dimensioning Standards: **ANSI**

Units: **INCHES** – 3 Decimals

Tools Needed:

Temporary Axis	Plane	Edit Component
Spline	Swept Boss/Base	Mass Properties

1. Opening an assembly document:

- Click **File / Open**.

- Browse to the Training Files folder and open a part document named: **Motor Assembly.sldasm**

- This assembly document has 3 components in it and they have been fully constrained with mates.

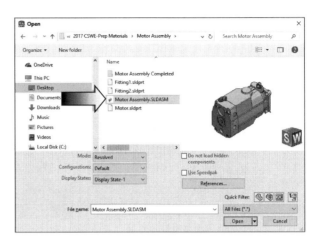

- This challenge will test your skills on building a new component in the context of an assembly, or Top-Down Assembly.

- Enable the **Temporary Axis** from the Hide/Show Items drop down.

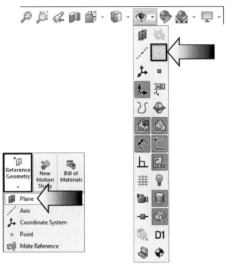

2. Creating a new plane:

- Switch to the Assembly tab and select: **Reference-Geometry / Plane**.

- For First Reference, select the **Axis** as noted.

- For Second Reference, select the **Top** plane from the Feature tree.

- Click **OK**.

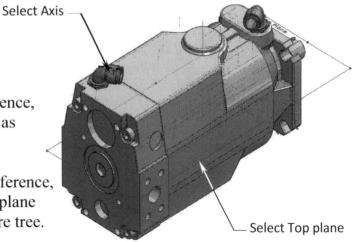

3. Creating a new component:

- Click the Insert Component's drop down arrow and select: **New Part**.

- The mouse cursor changes to a "Green-Checkmark," select the **new plane** (Plane1) from the Feature tree. This creates an Inplace reference between the new part and the Plane1, in the context of an assembly.

Select Plane1

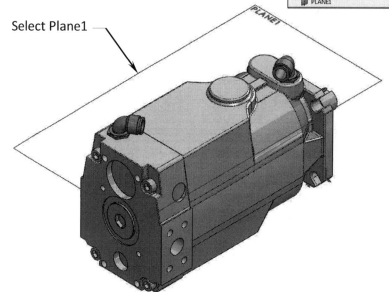

- A new component is created on the Feature tree. The Blue color represents the active part in the assembly and it is available for editing.

- A **new sketch** is created on the Plane1 automatically.

- Sketch a line from the center of each fitting as noted. Ensure that the lines are **Coincident** to the ends of the fitting and also **Concentric** with their centers.

Add line

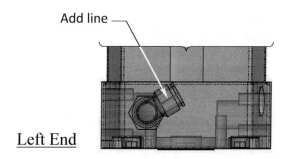

Left End

Add line

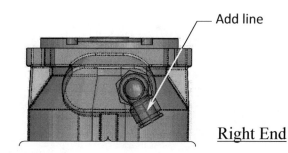

Right End

6-4

- Sketch a **2-Point Spline** to connect the two lines that were created in the last step.

- By using only two spline points you can easily manipulate the spline and still get a very smooth curve from it in the end.

- Drag the spline handles outwards, approximately as shown above.

- Add a **Tangent** relation between the Spline and one of the lines.

- Apply the same **Tangent** relation to the other side.

- The next step is to join the 3 entities into one.

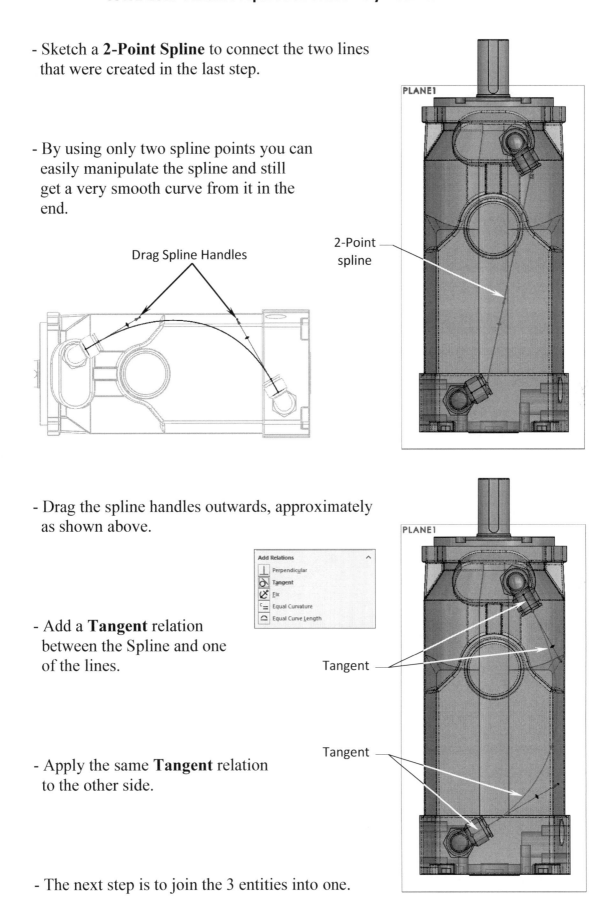

4. Creating a Fit Spline:

- The Fit Spline tool fits sketch segments to a spline. It is parametrically linked to underlying geometry so that changes to the geometry update the spline.

- Select the **Spline** and the **2 Lines**.

- Click: **Tools / Spline Tools / Fit Spline**.

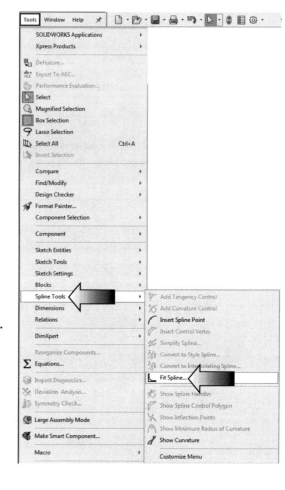

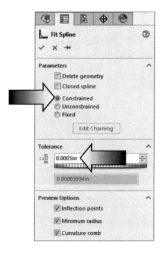

- Click the **Constrained** option.

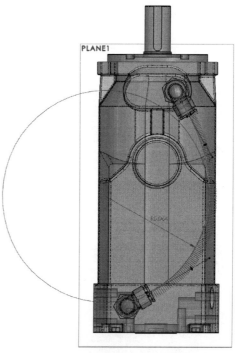

- Enter **.0005in** for Tolerance (arrow).

- Click **OK**. The 3 selected entities are joined into a spline.

6-6

5. Creating a new plane:

- We will use the "traditional method" to create the sweep feature, that way both circles (OD & ID) can be used at the same time to sweep along the path.

- Select **Reference Geometry / Plane**.

- Select the **line** on one side and click its **end point**.

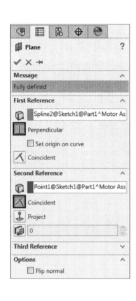

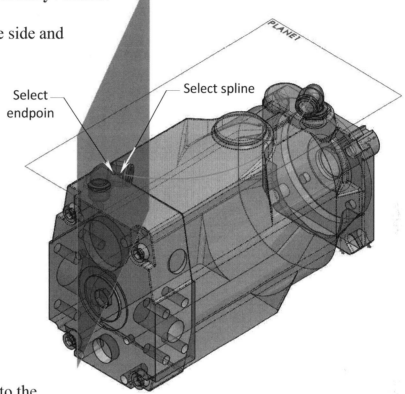

- A new plane normal to the line and coincident to the endpoint is created.

6. Sketching the sweep profile:

- Select the **new plane** and open a new sketch.

- Sketch **2 circles** that are coincident to the left end of the line. (OD = Ø.640, ID = Ø.520).

- **Exit** the sketch.

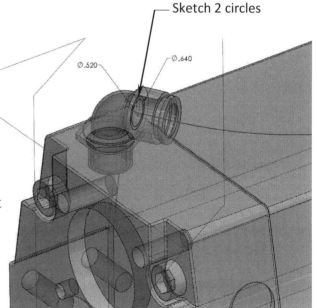

7. Creating the sweep:

- Change to the **Features** tab.

- Press **Swept Boss/Base**.

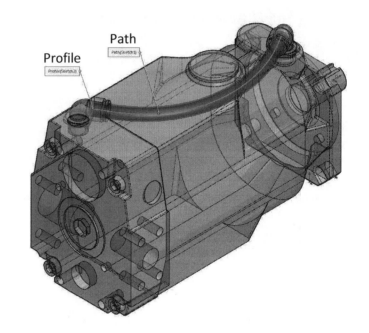

- For Sweep Path, select the sketch of the **Fit-Spline**.

- For Sweep Profile, select the sketch of the **Circles**.

- The preview graphics show the sweep feature is being generated.

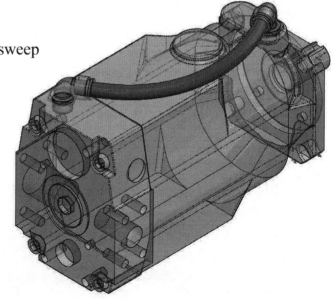

- Click **OK**.

- Compare your swept feature with the one shown here.

CSWE 2017 | Exam Preparation | Assembly Modifications

8. Assigning material:

- Click-off the **Edit Component** button to exit the part mode.

- Expand the **new part** (Part1) from the Feature tree.

- Right click the Material option and select **Copper** (arrow).

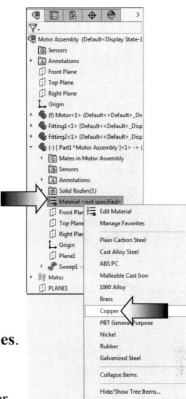

9. Calculating the mass:

- Change to the **Evaluate** tab and click **Mass Properties**.

- Locate the **Center Of Mass** of the assembly and enter it here:

X = _____

Y = _____

Z = _____

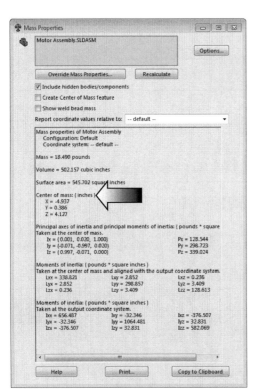
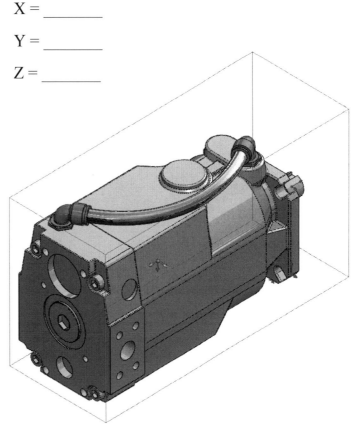

10. Saving your work:

- Save your work as **Motor Assembly (Completed).sldasm**

- Close all documents.

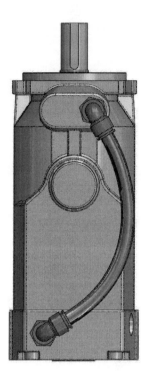
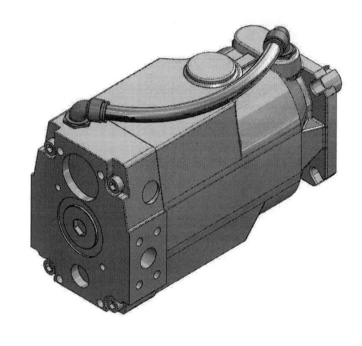

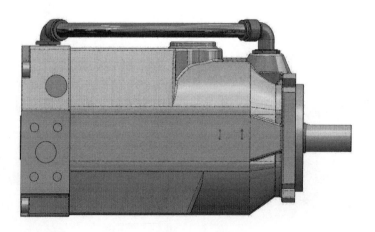

CHAPTER 7

Combine Common

CSWE Exam Preparation
Combine Common

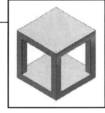 

When working with a multibody part, you can combine multiple solid bodies to create a single-bodied part or another multibody part.

The combine command offers three different options:

* The Combine-Add option combines multiple bodies to create a single body.

* The Combine-Subtract subtracts one or more bodies from another body.

* The Combine-Common creates a body defined by the intersection of multiple bodies.

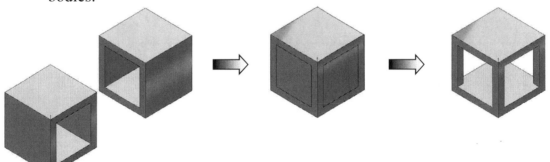

(You cannot combine two separate parts in the part level. To combine two or more parts, insert them into an assembly document and 'Join' them instead.)

This chapter will guide you through the use of the Combine-Common option. Two solid bodies will be created overlapping each other. The Combine-Common will be used to remove all material except that which overlaps, and the Volume of the resulted body is calculated as the answer to the question for this challenge.

CSWE Exam Preparation
Combine Common

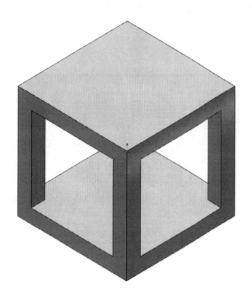

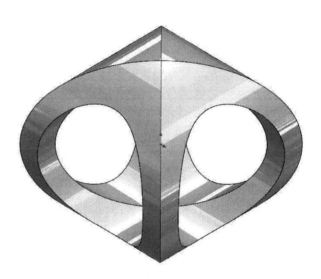

Dimensioning Standards: **ANSI**

Units: **INCHES** – 3 Decimals

Tools Needed:

 Center Rectangle   Circle   Offset Entities

 Extruded Boss/Base   Combine   Mass Properties

Using Combine Common Part 1

1. Starting a new part document:

- Click **File / New**.

- Select the **Part** template (arrow) and click **OK**.

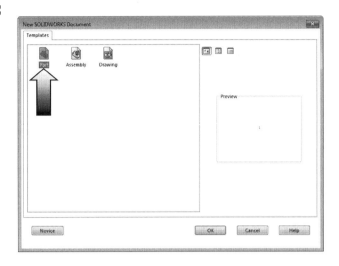

- We will build this part from scratch so that you will get to review the use of the Combine-Common option.

2. Creating the first solid body:

- Select the Front plane and open a **new sketch**.

- Sketch a **Center-Rectangle** as shown.

- Center the rectangle around the origin.

- Add the width and the height dimensions.

- The sketch should be fully defined at this point.

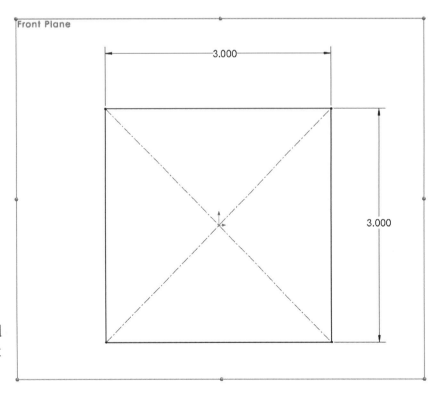

- Highlight the rectangle and click **Offset Entities**.

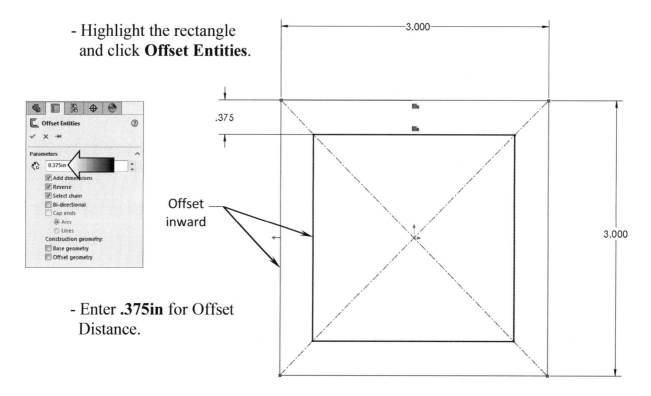

- Enter **.375in** for Offset Distance.

- Enable the **Reverse** checkbox to place the new entities on the inside.

- The sketch should remain fully defined.

- Switch to the **Features** tool tab and click **Extruded Boss/Base**.

- Select the **Mid-Plane** type.

- Enter **3.00in** for extrude depth.

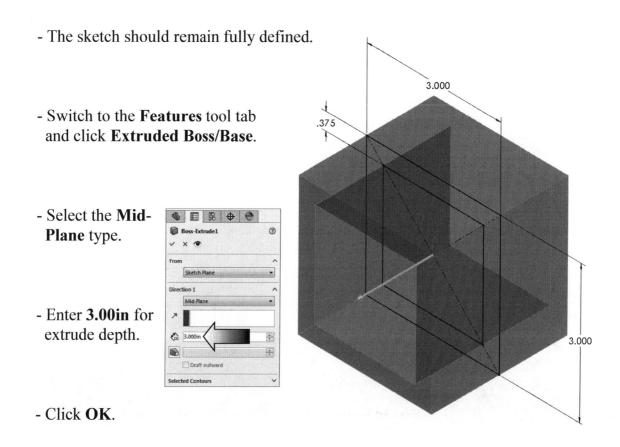

- Click **OK**.

3. Creating the second solid body:

- Select the Right plane and open a **new sketch**.

- Either copy from the previous sketch or re-create the same Center-Rectangle once again.

- Also create an offset of .375in from the same rectangle. Place the new entities on the inside.

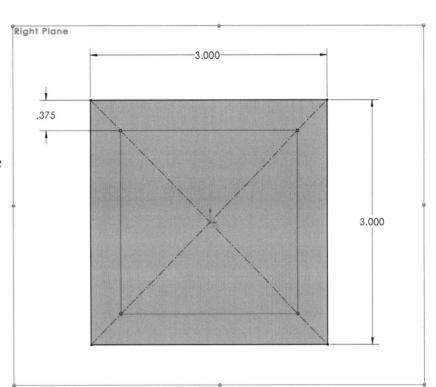

- Click **Extrude Boss/Base**.

- Select the **Mid-Plane** type and enter **3.00in.** for depth.

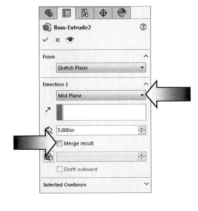

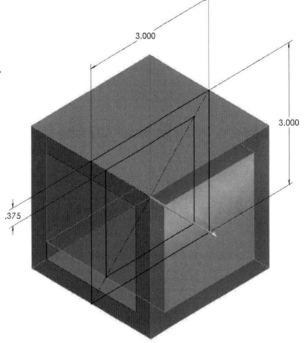

- Clear the **Merge Result** checkbox (arrow).

- Click **OK**. There should be two solid bodies in this model at this point.

4. Creating a Combine-Common body:

- The option Combine-Common removes all material except that which overlaps.

- In a multibody part, you can create a body defined by the intersection of multiple bodies. You can only combine bodies contained within one multibody part file.

- Select: **Insert / Features / Combine** (arrow).

- Click the **Common** option (arrow).

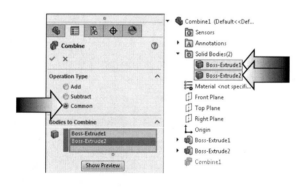

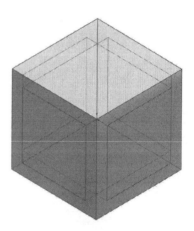

- Expand the Solid Bodies folder on the Feature tree and select the **two extruded bodies** (arrows).

- Click the **Preview** button to see the preview graphic of the intersection between the two bodies.

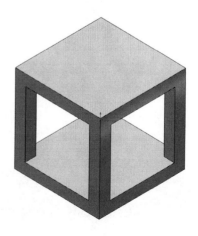

- Click **OK**.

5. Finding the volume of the new body:

- Change to the **Evaluate** tab.

- Click **Mass Property** .

- Locate the Volume for this part and enter it here: _____ Cubic Inches.

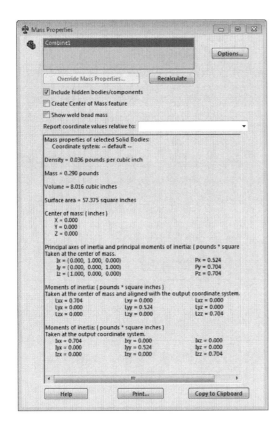

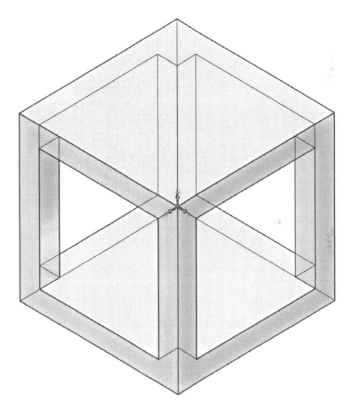

- Save the part file as **Combine1**.

- Close this document.

Using Combine Common Part 2

1. Starting a new part document:

- Click **File / New**.

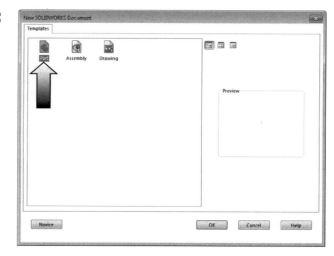

- Select the **Part** template (arrow) and click **OK**.

- The second half of this chapter is very similar to the first, but we will be using cylinders instead of squares. Cylindrical features are much more difficult to predict the outcome, or what the intersection between the two bodies would look like, compared to rectangular features.

2. Creating the first solid body:

- Select the Front plane and open a **new sketch**.

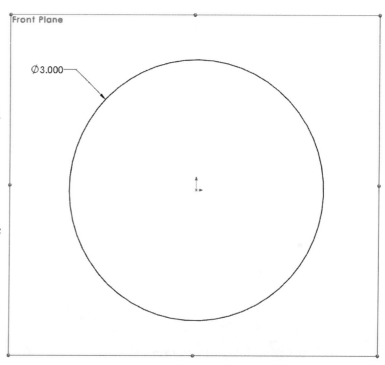

- Sketch a **Circle** centered on the origin.

- Add the **3.00in** diameter dimension to fully define this sketch.

- Remain in the sketch mode for the next step.

- Select the sketch circle and click **Convert Entities**.

- Enter **.375in** for Offset Distance. Place the new entity on the <u>inside</u>.

- The sketch should still be fully defined at this point.

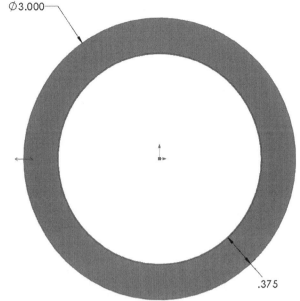

- Switch to the **Features** tab and click **Extruded Boss/Base**.

- Select the **Mid Plane** type.

- Enter **3.00in** for extrude depth

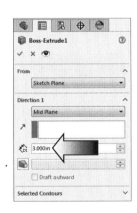

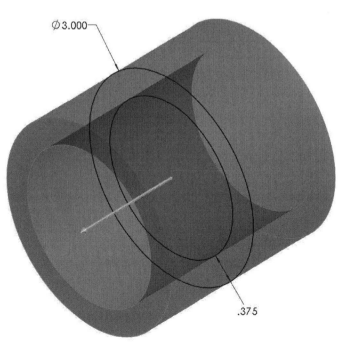

- Click **OK**.

- The first solid body is created.

3. Creating the second solid body:

- Select the Right plane and open a **new sketch**.

- Sketch another Circle, also center it on the origin.

- Add the **3.00in** diameter dimension to fully define this sketch.

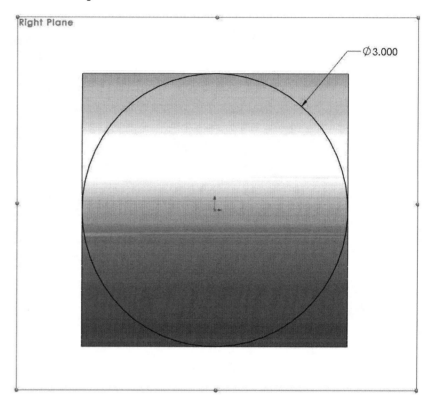

- Switch to the **Features** tab and click **Extruded Boss/Base**.

- Select the **Mid Plane** type and enter **3.00in** for extrude depth.

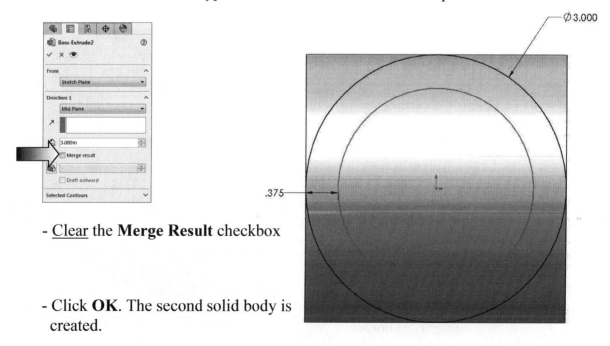

- Clear the **Merge Result** checkbox

- Click **OK**. The second solid body is created.

4. Creating a Combine-Common body:

- Select: **Insert / Features / Combine**.

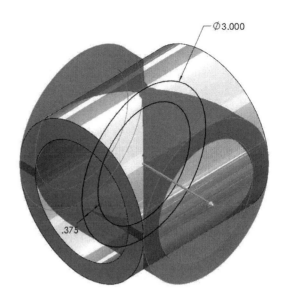

- Click the **Common** option.

- Expand the Solid Bodies folder on the Feature tree and select the **two extruded bodies** (arrows).

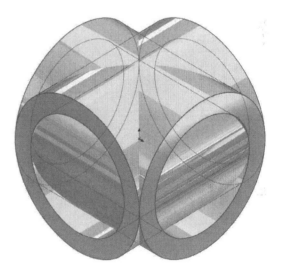

- Click the **Preview** button to see the preview graphics of the intersection between the two bodies.

- Click **OK**.

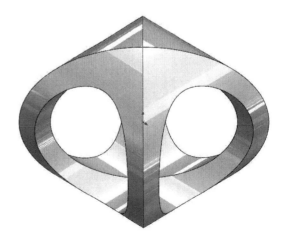

- The intersection, or the common area between the two solid bodies is created.

5. Finding the volume of the new body:

- Change to the **Evaluate** tab.

- Click **Mass Property** .

- Locate the Volume for this part and enter it here: _____ Cubic Inches.

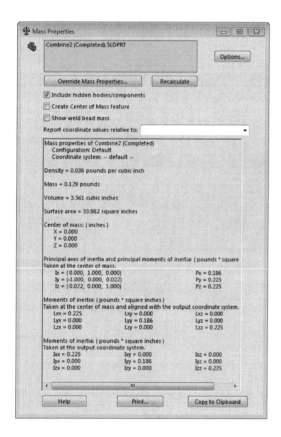

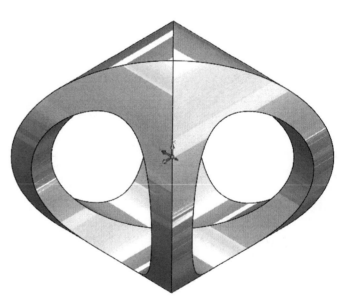

- Save the part file as **Combine2**.

- Close all documents.

Using Combine Common Part 3

1. Opening a part document:

- Click **File / Open**.

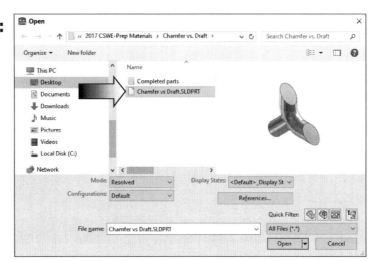

- Browse to the Training Files folder and open the part document named: **Chamfer vs Draft.sldprt**.

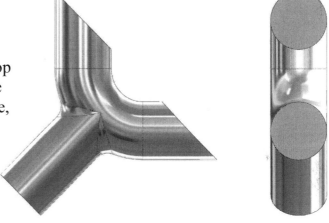

- This part is a solid model. The top and right sides of the model have been trimmed to a 45° taper angle, and the bottom is flat.

- The challenge is to create a chamfer that runs <u>evenly</u> around the edges of the left and right sides of the model as shown below.

Before

After

2. Adding an Angle and Depth chamfer:

- Let's take a look at some of the chamfer options and see which one can produce the result that we are looking for.

- Click **Chamfer** under the Fillet command

- Use the default **Angle and Depth** option (arrow).

- Enter **1.00in** for Depth and leave the Angle at **45°**.

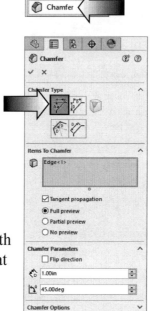
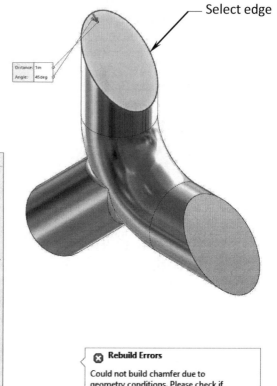

Select edge

- Click **OK**.
An error message appears indicating the chamfer cannot be built.

3. Changing to a Distance and Distance chamfer:

- Select the **Distance and Distance** chamfer option (arrow).

- This option is used to define the chamfer with two depth dimensions, no angle is needed.

- Select **Symmetric** under Chamfer-Parameters (arrow).

- Leave the Depth at **1.00in** and click **OK**.

- The preview graphic shows the chamfer is being applied unevenly around the selected edge.

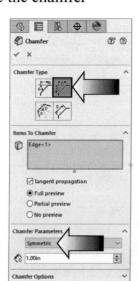
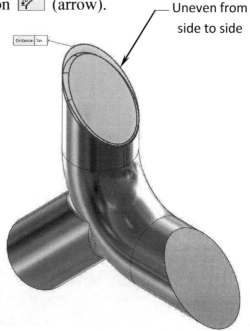

Uneven from side to side

4. Creating an Offset Face chamfer:

- Select the **Offset Face** chamfer option (arrow).

- Keep the Chamfer Depth at **1.00in**.

- Select the **face** as indicated.

- The preview graphic shows the chamfers are being applied <u>unevenly</u> around the edge of the selected face.

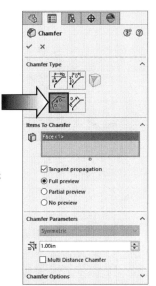
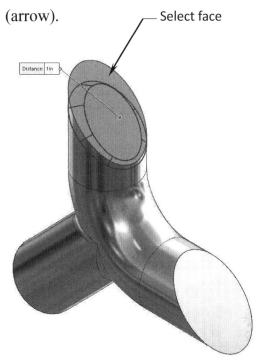

5. Changing to a Face-Face chamfer:

- Change to the **Face-Face** chamfer type (arrow).

- This option blends a chamfer between non-adjacent, non-continuous faces.

- For Face Set 1, select the **top face** of the model as noted.

- For Face Set 2, select the **side face** indicated.

- Keep the Chamfer Depth at **1.00in**.

- The preview graphic shows the chamfer is being applied <u>unevenly</u> around the edge of the model once again.

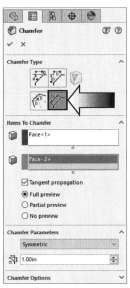
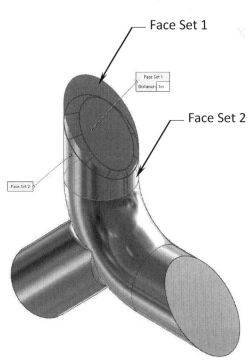

6. Creating a Split Line:

- Split Line is a different approach, but can produce the result that we need.

- Open a new sketch on the **Front** plane.

- Press **Control+1** to change to the front orientation.

- Sketch a **Line** and a **Centerline** as indicated.

- Add the relations and dimensions as shown.

- Switch to the **Features** tool tab and select: **Curves / Split Line** (arrow).

- Select the **Projection** option (arrow).

- The Current Sketch should be selected automatically.

- For Faces to Split, select the **2 faces** as noted.

- Click **OK**.

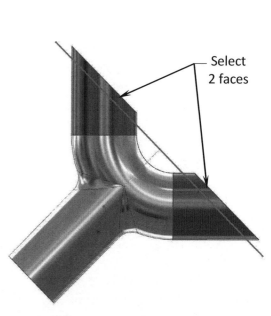

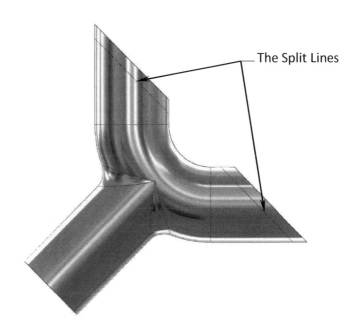

The Split Lines

7. Creating a Parting Line Draft:

- Select the **Draft** command from the Features tab.

- Click the **Parting Line** option (arrow).

- For Draft Angle, enter **45°**.

- For Direction of Pull, select the **face** as noted.

- For Parting Lines, select the **two edges** on the two sides as indicated.

- Click **OK**.

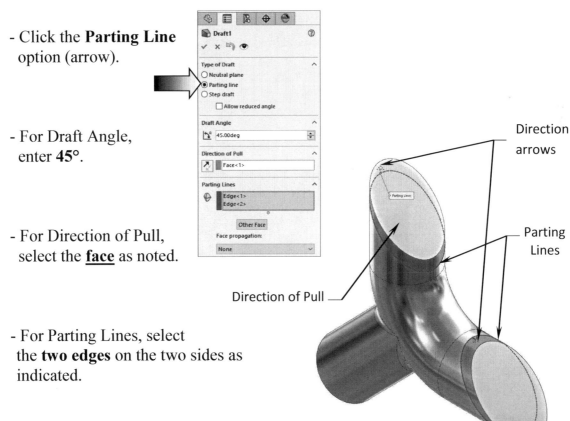

7-17

8. Assigning material:

- Right click the material option and select: **1060 Alloy** (arrow).

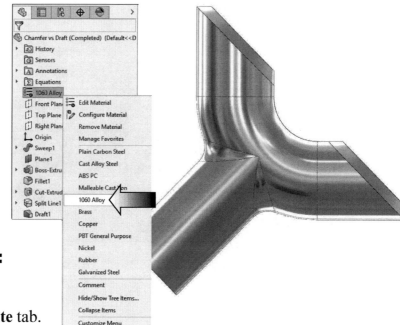

9. Calculating the mass:

- Switch to the **Evaluate** tab.

- Locate the mass of the part and enter it here: _____ lbs.

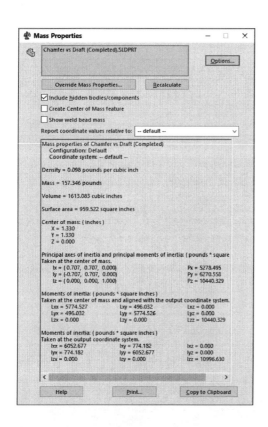

- Save your work and close all documents.

CHAPTER 8

Part Modifications

CSWE Exam Preparation
Part Modifications

This chapter discusses different methods to solve the challenges in the following areas:

* Modifying geometry of the initial part to create a more complex part

* Deleting and patching features

* Updating parameters and dimension sizes

* Modifying parameters on the part at different stages while maintaining all other dimensions and design intent

* Converting a single solid body into a multibody part

* Mass property analysis

- There are many methods that you can use to create or modify the models in SOLIDWORKS, but the methods that you will learn from this chapter are just some of techniques provided to give you an idea of what to expect in the actual challenge.

- It is recommended that you should practice with the materials and to explore the different ways to create or to modify the model, and then use the one that you most comfortable with to solve the challenges.

- This chapter offers three different techniques for revising the models while maintaining their relationships and design intents.

CSWE Exam Preparation
Part Modifications

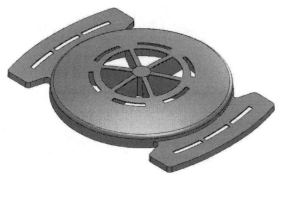

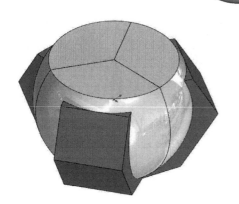

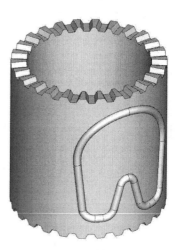

Dimensioning Standards: **ANSI**

Units: **INCHES** – 3 Decimals

Tools Needed:

 Convert Entities Extruded Boss Extruded Cut

 Delete Face Fillet Circular Pattern

Part Modifications - Challenge 1 of 5

1. Opening a part document:

- Select **File / Open**.

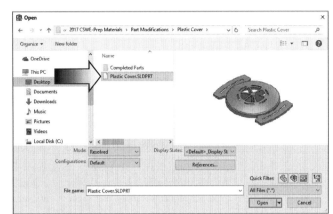

- Browse to the Training Files folder and open a part document named: **Plastic Cover.sldprt**.

- This challenge tests your skills on modifying features in a part.

- The two fillets in this model have been suppressed (arrow) to help improve the computer performance. They do not affect the modifications of the part

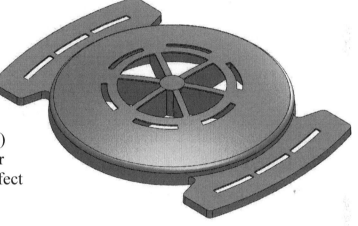

- After the changes are completed the fillets will be unsuppressed prior to calculating the final mass of the part.

2. Modifying the pattern angle:

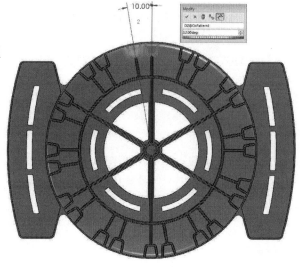

- Double click the feature **CirPattern1** (arrow) and locate the **10°** angular dimension.

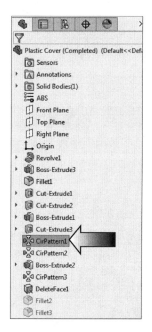

- Change the angle from **10°** to **12°**.

- Press **Rebuild** .

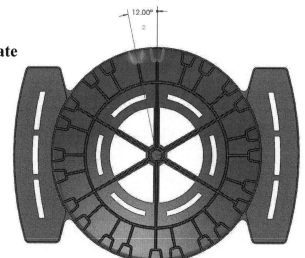

- Switch to the **Evaluate** tab and click **Mass Properties**.

- Enter the **Mass** here:

_____ lbs.

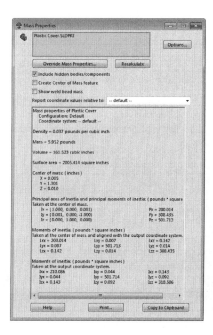

3. Changing the pattern angle:

- Double click the feature **CirPattern1** once again.

- Change the pattern angle from **12°** to **15°**.

- Press **Rebuild**.

- **Un-suppress** the **two fillets** from the Feature tree (arrow).

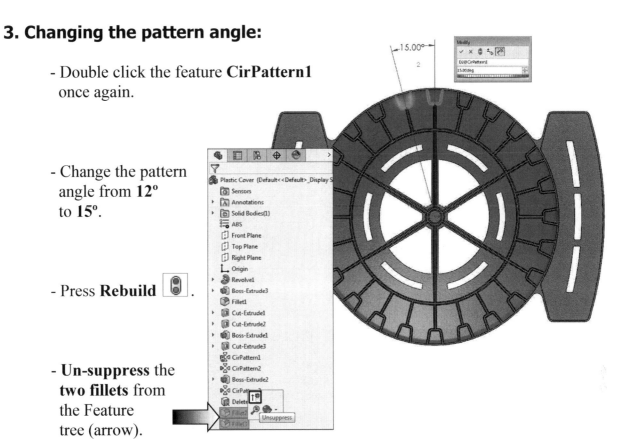

4. Calculating the final mass:

- Locate the **mass** of the part and enter it here:

  _____ lbs.

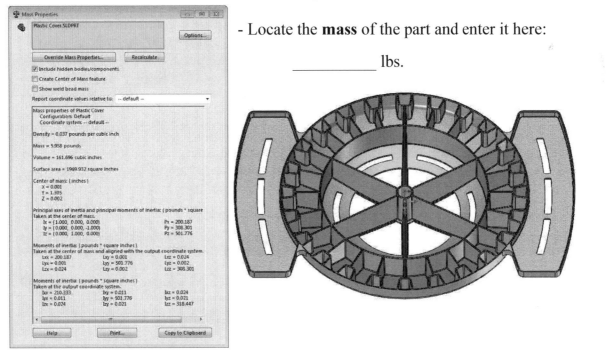

- Save your work as **Plastic Cover (completed).sldprt**

Part Modifications – Challenge 2 of 5

1. Opening a part document:

- Select **File / Open**.

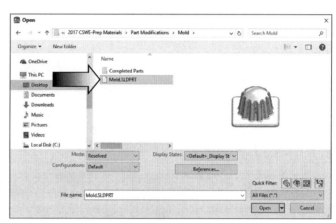

- Browse to the Training Files folder and open a part document named: **Mold.sldprt**.

- This challenge will test your skills on modifying the geometry of a model while maintaining the existing relationships of all features.

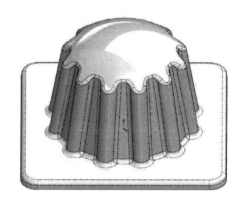

Before

- You are also expected to repair any errors while keeping all sketches fully defined.

- Keep in mind that there is always more than one way to create or change the models using SOLIDWORKS. The method shown here is just one of techniques provided to give you an idea of what to expect in the actual challenge, you may want to explore different ways to revise the model and use the one that you are most comfortable with.

After

2. Filling the hollow cavity:

- In some cases it would be much easier to work with a solid model than a thin walled. We will fill the shell feature to revert the model back into a solid body.

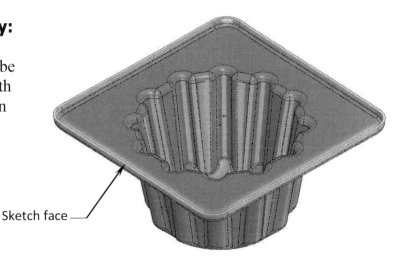

Sketch face

- Select the bottom **face** of the model and open a new sketch.

- Right click on one of the outer edges and pick: **Select-Tangency** (arrow).

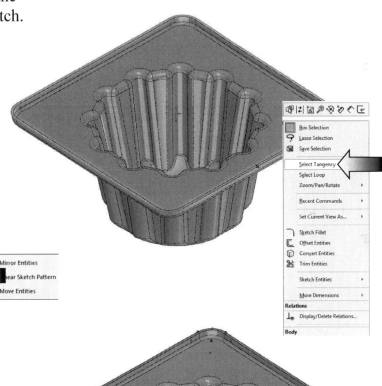

- Click **Convert-Entities** from the Sketch toolbar.

- All selected edges are converted into new sketch entities.

- Switch to the **Features** tool tab.

- Select **Extruded Boss/Base**.

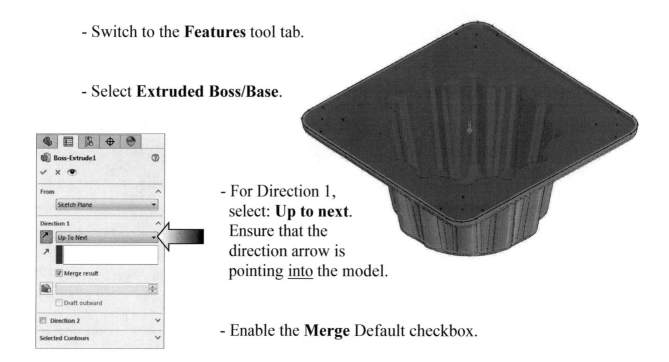

- For Direction 1, select: **Up to next**. Ensure that the direction arrow is pointing <u>into</u> the model.

- Enable the **Merge** Default checkbox.

3. Deleting the first group of fillets:

- Change to the **Surfaces** tab.

- Select the **Delete Face** command (arrow) and click the **Delete and Patch** option.

- Select the **12 faces** on the four sides of the base. DO NOT select the 4 planar faces as noted.

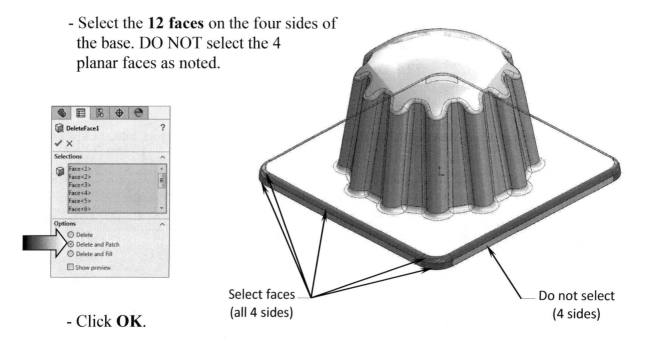

- Click **OK**.

8-8

- The fillets on the base are removed. Your model should look like the the one shown here.

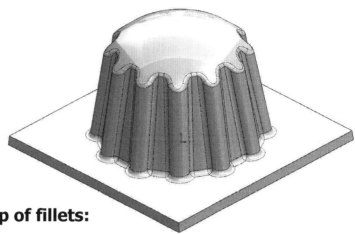

4. Removing the second group of fillets:

- Select the **Delete Face** command again.

- Click the **Delete and Patch** option.

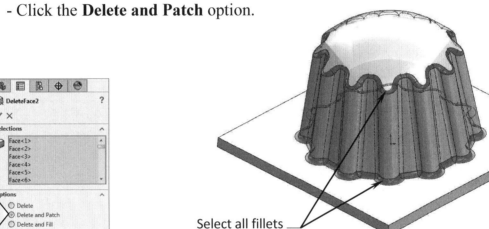

Select all fillets on top & bottom

- Select **all fillets** on the top and bottom of the raised feature in the middle. (There should 96 faces total).

- Click **OK**.

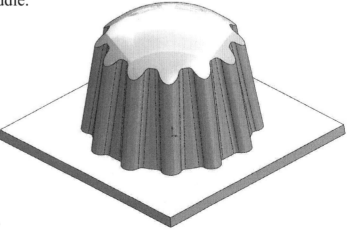

- The selected fillets are removed. Your model should look like the one shown here.

8-9

5. Removing the third group of fillets:

- Select the **Delete Face** command once again.

- The **Delete and Path** option should still be selected.

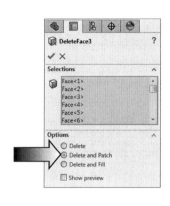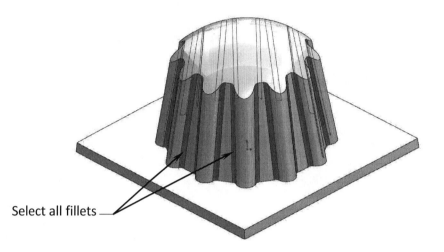

Select all fillets

- Select all the fillets that are left in the part.
  (There should be 24 faces total.)

- Click **OK**.

- We had to delete the fillets in three separate
  steps because some of the fillets need
  to be connected to the adjacent faces.
  The removal of the fillets may
  fail if we were to delete them
  all at the same time.

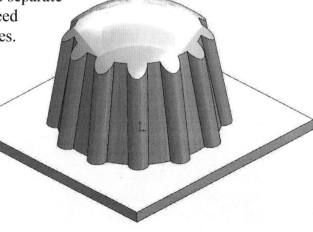

- Your model should look
  like the one shown here.

6. Modifying the base:

- Select the **Right** plane and open a new sketch.

- Sketch the profile shown below. Add dimensions / relations to fully define the sketch.

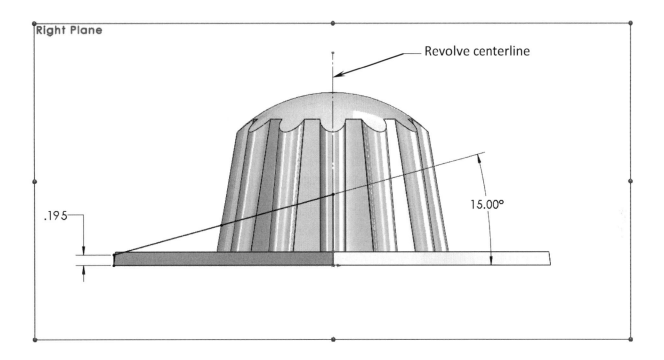

- Change to the **Features** tab and click **Revolved Boss/Base**.

- Use the default **Blind** type and **360°** revolve angle.

- Keep the box **Merge Result** checked.

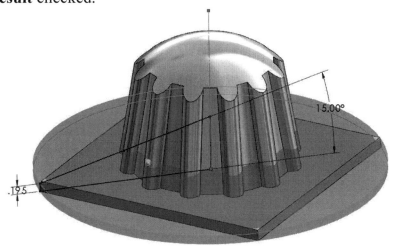

- Click **OK**.

- The revolved features left some "slivers" that will get cleaned up in the next step.

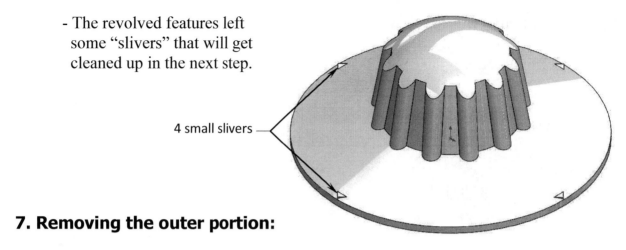

4 small slivers

7. Removing the outer portion:

- Next, we will remove the outer portion of the base.

- Select the **Top** plane and open a new sketch.

- Sketch a **Center-Rectangle** and add the dimensions shown to fully define it.

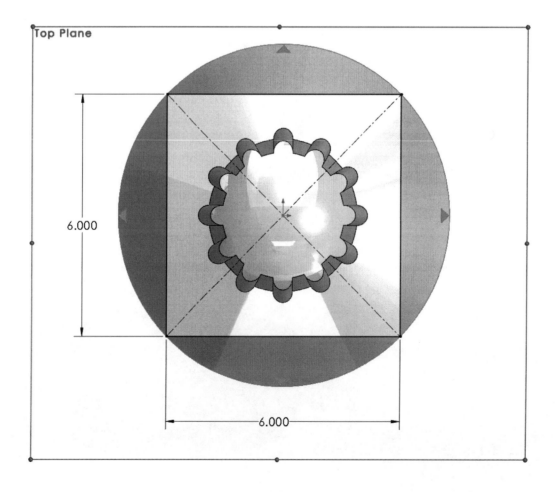

- Switch to the **Features** tab.

- Press **Extruded Cut**.

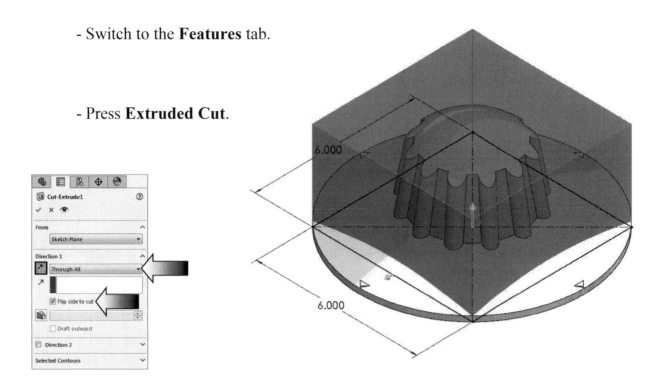

- Select **Through All** and click **Reverse** direction.

- Enable the **Flip Side To Cut** checkbox (arrow).

- Click **OK**.

- The base is trimmed to a square shape and the four slivers are removed.

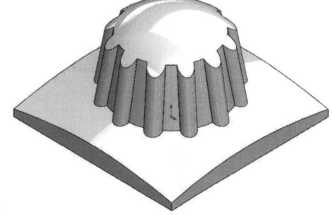

- Your models should look like the one shown here at this point.

8. Adding fillets to the base:

- Select the **Fillet** command from the Features tab.

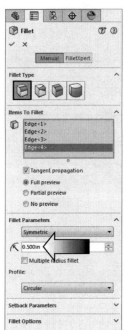
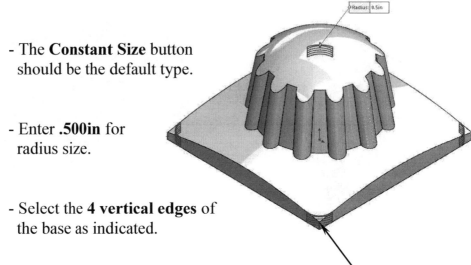

- The **Constant Size** button should be the default type.

- Enter **.500in** for radius size.

- Select the **4 vertical edges** of the base as indicated.

- Click **OK**.

Select 4 edges

9. Adding fillets to other features:

- Click the **Fillet** command again.

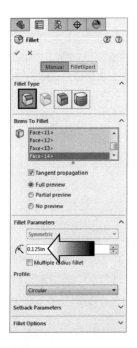

- Use the default **Constant-Size** radius option.

- Enter **.125in** for radius size.

- Select the **faces** as noted to add the fillets.

- Click **OK**.

Select faces (all around)

- All edges in the model should be filleted, except for the bottom edges.

10. Shelling the part:

- Select the **Shell** command from the Features tab.

- For Thickness, enter **.060in**.

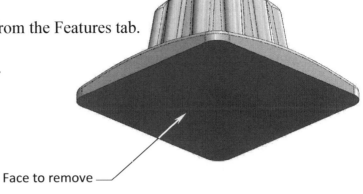

Face to remove

- For Faces to Remove, select the **bottom face** of the model.

- Click **OK**.

- The model is shelled and a constant wall thickness is kept all around.

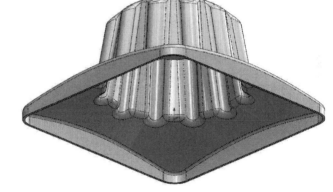

11. Creating a section view:

- Click **Section View** command on the Heads-Up View toolbar.

- Use the default **Front** plane.

- Enter **45°** in the X Rotation box (arrow) to create a cut at 45°.

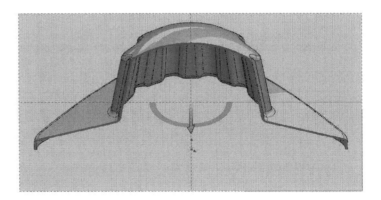

- Click **OK**.

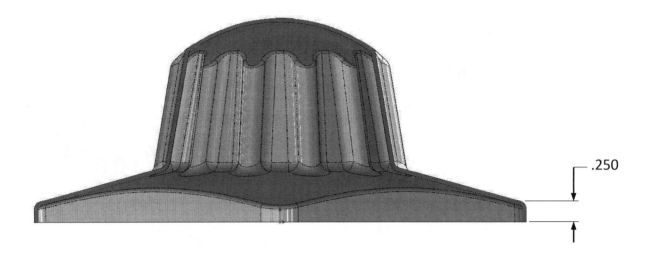

- Change to the Front orientation (Control+1) and press the Left arrow key three times to look normal to the sectioned surface.

- Measure from the bottom edge to the Virtual intersection as shown. One way to do this is to create a drawing view from the model, create an intersection point (hold Control select the two lines and click the Point command).

12. Assigning material:

- Right click the **Material** option on the Feature tree.

- Select **1060 Alloy** from the list.

- Mass Properties can now be calculated for this model.

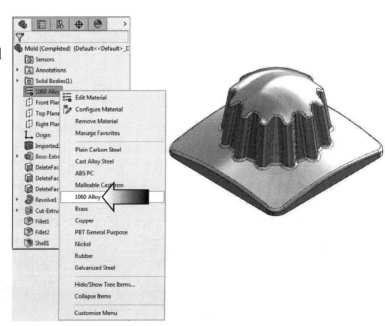

13. Calculating the final mass:

- Switch to the **Evaluate** tab.

- Click **Mass Properties**.

- Locate the **mass** of the part and enter it here: _____ lbs.

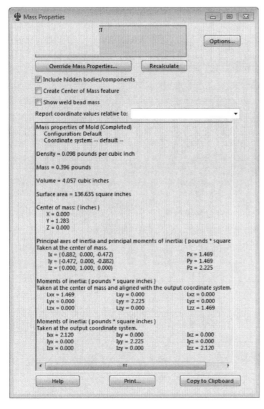

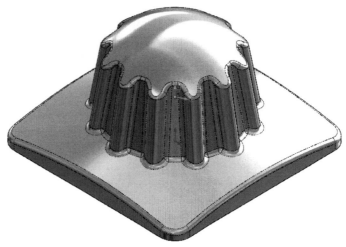

14. Saving your work:

- Save your work as **Mold (Completed).sldprt**.

- Close all documents.

Part Modifications – Challenge 3 of 5

1. Opening a part document:

- Select **File / Open**.

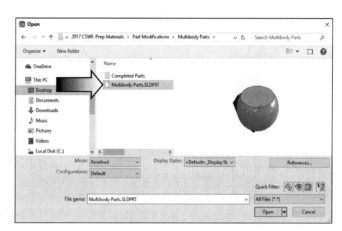

- Browse to the Training Files folder and open a part document named: **Multibody Parts.sldprt**

- This challenge will examine your skills on converting a single body into a multibody part.

- This model was imported and has no feature history.

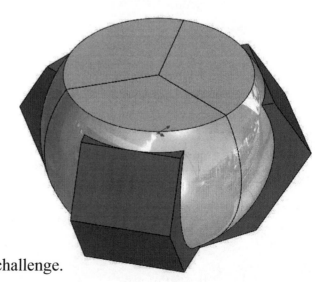

- There is only one solid body at this point. We will need to create a cut and remove the unwanted portions of the part, the left over body will get patterned circularly three times to create the multibody part. The material will be assigned to the part and the final mass can be calculated as the answer to this challenge.

2. Creating a cut feature:

- Open a new sketch top most <u>face</u>.

- Sketch the profile as shown on the right.

- Add dimensions and relations to fully define the sketch.

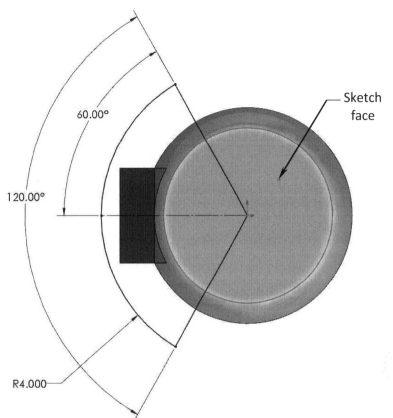

- Switch to the **Features** tab and click **Extruded Cut**.

- Select the **Through All** type.

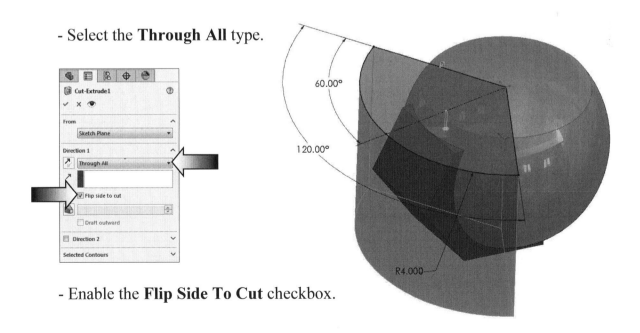

- Enable the **Flip Side To Cut** checkbox.

- Click **OK**.

8-19

3. Creating a circular pattern of the body:

- Select the **Circular Pattern** command below the Linear Pattern drop down.

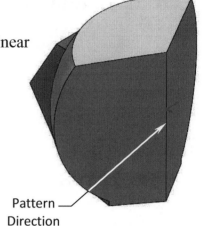
Pattern Direction

- For pattern Direction, select the **edge** as noted.

- Enable the **Equal Spacing** checkbox.

- Keep the angle at **360°** and enter **3** for number of instances.

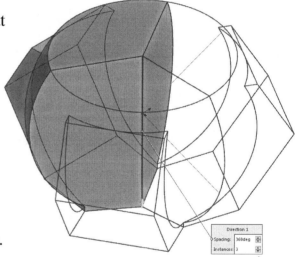

- Enable the **Bodies** checkbox (arrow).

- Select the **solid body** either from the graphics area or from the Feature tree.

- The preview graphics shows three bodies are being created.

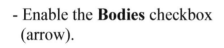

- Click **OK**.

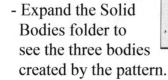

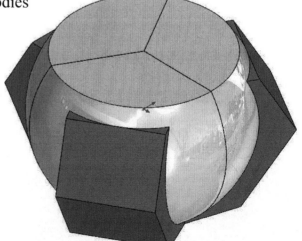

- Expand the Solid Bodies folder to see the three bodies created by the pattern.

4. Assigning material:

- Right click the **Material** option from the Feature tree and select: **Edit Material**.

- Expand the **Plastics** folder and select: **ABS**.

- Click **Apply** and **Close** to exit.

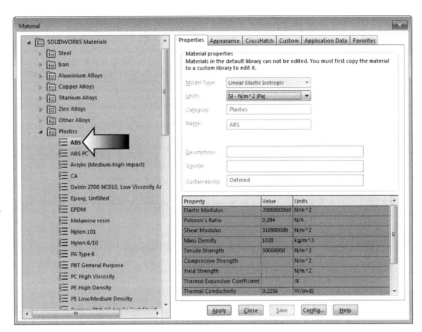

5. Calculating the final mass:

- Change to the **Evaluate** tab.

- Locate the **mass** of the part and enter it here:

  _____ lbs.

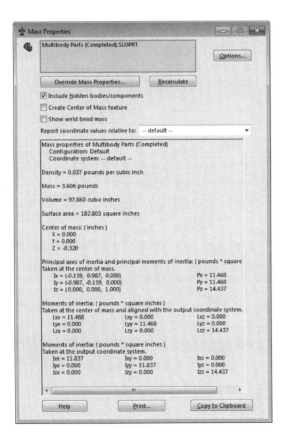

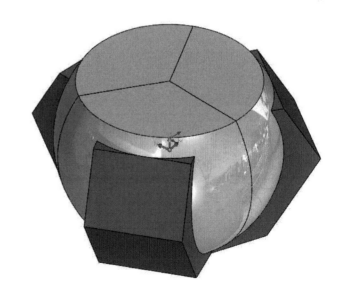

8-21

Part Modifications – Challenge 4 of 5

1. Opening a part document:

- Click **File / Open**.

- Browse to the Training Files folder open the part document named: **Part Modifications**.

- This is an imported part, there are no features on the tree except for the Imported1.

- The material has been pre-assigned as: **Aluminum 2014-T6**.

- The raised pattern will get deleted in the next couple of steps and replaced with a similar pattern. But first, we need to preserve the outline of the pattern for later use.

2. Converting the outline of the pattern:

- The Convert Entities command copies the selected geometry and projects onto the active plane.

- Select the **Right** plane and open a new sketch.

- Right click the edge indicated and pick: **Select Tangency**.

- The outline of the pattern is selected.

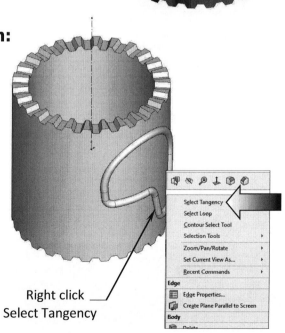

Right click
Select Tangency

- Click the **Convert Entities** command on the Sketch toolbar.

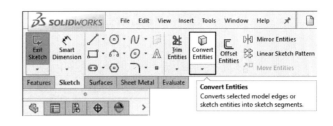

- The selected edges are converted to new sketch geometry, and they automatically become fully defined.

- The converted entities are related to the original geometry. When the original geometry is deleted, the converted entities will become dangling; so to overcome this issue, we will delete the On-Edge relations ahead of time.

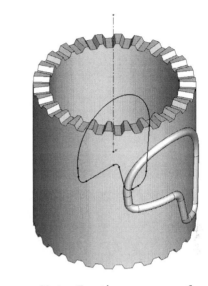

Note: For the purpose of the lesson, this sketch can be left under define.

- Click the **Display / Delete Relations** from the Sketch toolbar, set the filter to: <u>All In this Sketch</u> (arrow), and <u>delete</u> all On Edge relations from the properties tree.

- Complete the sketch by <u>mirroring</u> and <u>adding</u> the additional entities as shown.

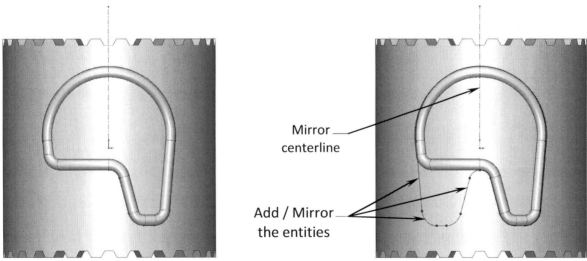

- **Exit** the sketch, we will come back to it in the next couple steps.

3. Removing the raised pattern:

- Select the Top plane and open a new sketch.

- Sketch **two circles** centered on the origin.

- Add two diameter dimensions to fully define the sketch.

Note: There are several ways to remove the raised feature, but the extruded cut option happens to be a little quicker than the others.

4. Extruding a cut:

- Switch to the **Features** toolbar.

- Click the **Extruded Cut** command.

- Select **Through All Both**.

*Use a line, an edge, or axis to change the extrude direction if needed.

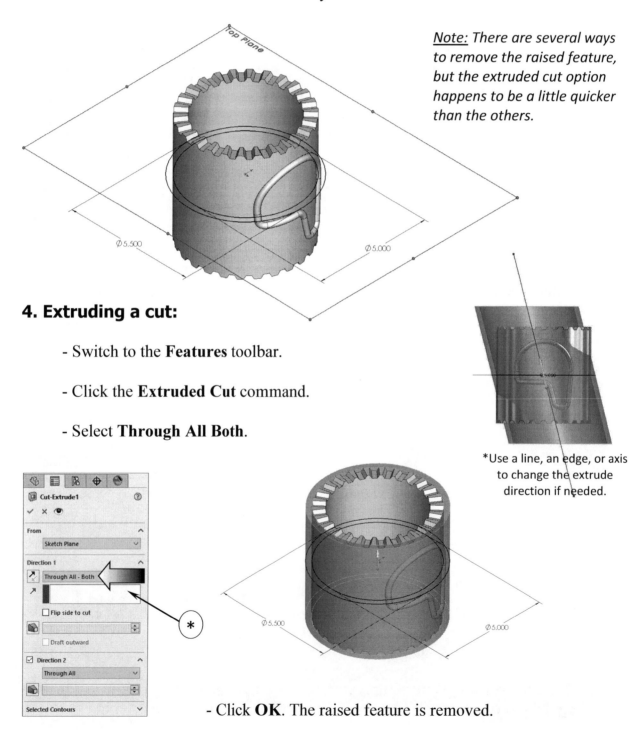

- Click **OK**. The raised feature is removed.

5. Creating the sweep path:

- From the Features toolbar, click the **Curves** button and select the **Project Curve** command from the list (arrow).

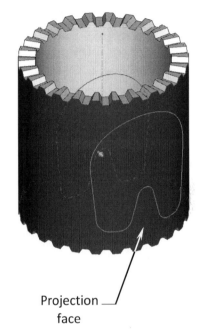

- Select the **Sketch on Faces** option (arrow).

- Under the section: Sketch To Project, select the **Sketch1** from the Feature tree or click it from the graphics area.

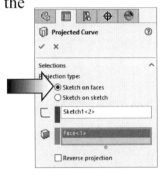

- Under the Projection Faces, select the **outer face** of the cylinder.

- The preview appears indicating the project curve is being created.

- Click **OK** to accept the projected curve.

Projection face

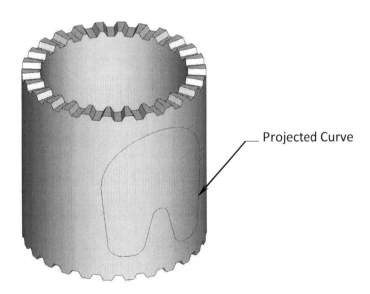

Projected Curve

- Rotate the view to verify the projection. The curve should be projected on the front of the cylinder.

8-25

6. Creating a swept feature:

- Switch to the **Features** tab.

- Select the **Swept Boss/Base** command.

- Click the **Circular Profile** option (arrow).

- Enter **.250in** for Diameter.

- For Path, select the **Projected-Curve**.

- Expand the Options section and select the following:

    * Follow Path.   * Show Preview.

    * Merge Tangent Faces.   * Merge Result.

- Click **OK**.

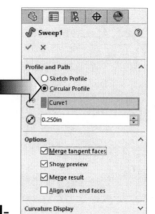

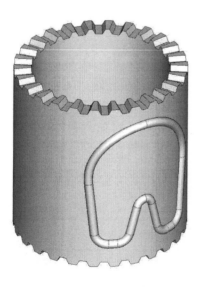
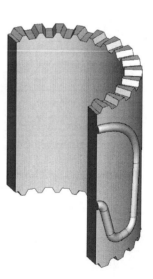

- The swept feature is recreated. The raised feature should be evenly swept along the path. Create a section view to check the result.

7. Calculating the mass:

- Click **Tools / Mass Properties**.

- Using three decimals, **enter the Mass of the part here:** _____ lbs.

- Click the Options button on top of the dialog box to change the number of decimal places and/or the units of the part.

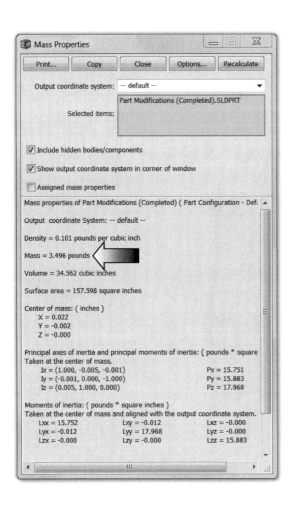

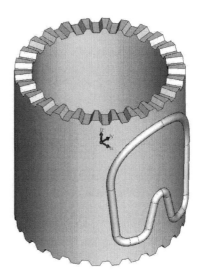

8. Saving your work:

- Click **File / Save As**.

- Enter **Part Modification Completed** for the name of the file.

- Click **Save**.

- Close the part document.

NOTE: Refer to the completed part saved in the Training Files folder for reference or to compare your results against it.

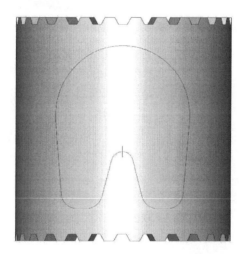

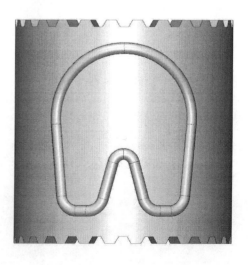

Part Modifications - Challenge 5 of 5

1. Opening a part document:

- Click **File / Open**.

- Browse to the Training Files folder and open the part document named: **Part Modifications_Exe**.

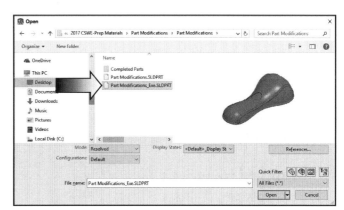

- This solid model has a circular feature in the middle where the label will be placed, and it needs to be changed to a rectangular shape.

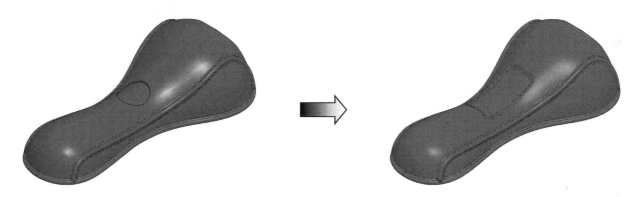

- This exercise will show one of the methods to accomplish that type of change.

2. Creating an Offset Surface:

- Switch to the Surfaces tool tab and select the **Surface Offset** command.

- Select the face of the circular cut out as noted to offset from.

- Enter **0** (zero) for offset distance. This surface will be used as one of the loft profiles to close off the cut out.

- Click **OK**.

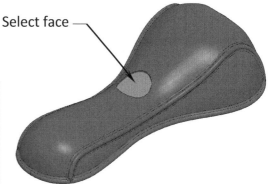

Select face

3. Creating a Surface Fill:

- Click the **Surface Fill** command from Surfaces tool tab.

- Select the upper edge as indicated.

- Change the fill type to **Tangent**.

- Enable the options **Apply to All Edges** and **Optimized Surfaces**.

- The mesh preview appears indicating that the new surface is being created.

- Click **OK**.

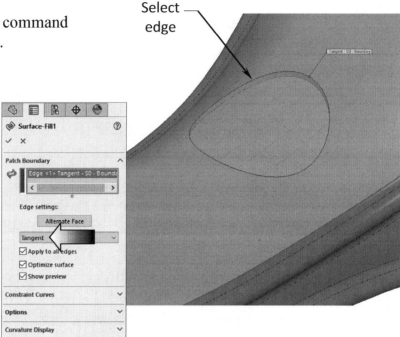

4. Creating a lofted feature:

- Switch to the Feature tool tab and select the **Lofted Boss-Base** command.

- From the FeatureManager tree, select both surfaces, the **Offset Surface** and the **Filled Surface**.

- Drag the connectors so that they are approximately vertical with one another.

- The mesh preview indicates the feature is being generated.

- Click **OK** to accept and exit the command.

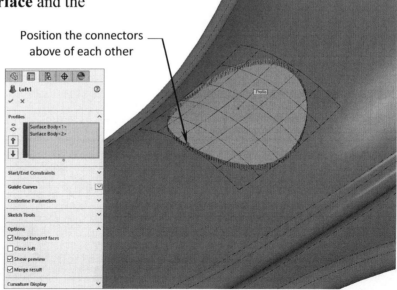

5. Creating the new cut profile:

- Select the Top plane and open a new sketch.

- Sketch a **Center-Rectangle** centered on the origin.

- Add the dimensions shown to fully define the sketch.

- Add the sketch fillets to the four corners.

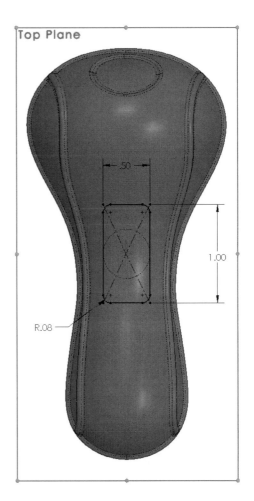

- Switch to the Features tool tab.

- Click **Extruded Cut**.

- Change the option under extrude **From** to **Offset**.

- Enter **1.00in** to extend the cut profile 1-inch away from its sketch plane.

- Under the **Direction1** section, select the **Offset From Surface** type.

- Select the face as indicated to offset from.

- Enter **.02in** for offset distance.

- Enable the **Reverse Offset** checkbox to cut into the part.

- Click **OK** to accept and exit out of the command.

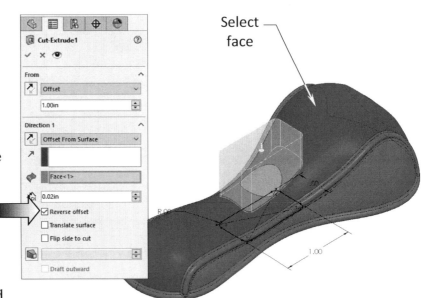

6. Creating the first .050" fillet:

- Click the **Fillet** command from the Feature tool tab.

- Use the default **Constant Radius** option.

- Enter **.05"** for radius size.

- Select the **outer edge** of the recess cut as noted.

- The Tangent Propagation checkbox should be selected by default.

- Click **OK**.

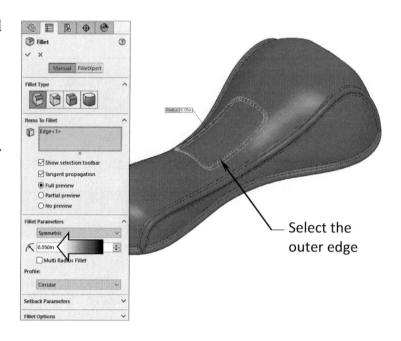

Select the outer edge

7. Creating the second .050" fillet:

- Click the **Fillet** command again or press the **Enter** key to repeat the previous command.

- Use the default fillet type and the same fillet value as the last one.

- Select one of the **inner edges** of the recess cut as indicated.

- Click **OK**.

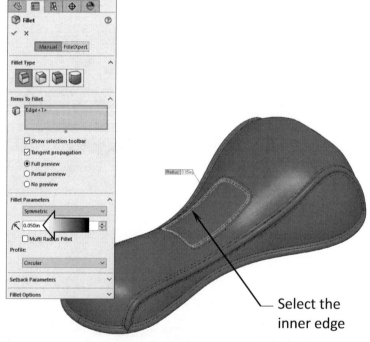

Select the inner edge

8. Saving your work:

- Click **File / Save As**.

- Enter **Part Modifications_Exe** for the name of the file.

- Press **Save** and close all documents.

CHAPTER 9

Cut with Surface

CSWE Exam Preparation
Cut with Surface

The Cut-With-Surface command removes the material of a solid or mutibody part. The direction of the cut can be toggled in or out using the reverse option.

When working with mutibody parts, an option called Feature Scope appears on the properties tree, allowing you to select the bodies that you want to cut.

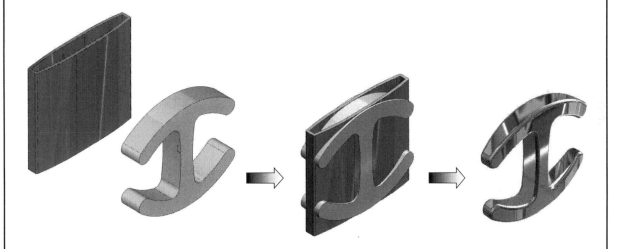

This lesson uses two independent components and each one consists of one solid body. After fully positioned, or mated, the two components will cause an interference by design.

We will use the top-down approach to create an offset surface from one of the parts, and use it to cut into the other. This is similar to the Boolean and subtraction options in most software, except we are going to create the cut using a surface that was derived or extracted from other components.

CSWE Exam Preparation
Cut with Surface

Dimensioning Standards: **ANSI**

Units: **INCHES** – 3 Decimals

Tools Needed:

 Edit Component   Offset Surface

 Hide/Show Component   Cut with Surface

1. Opening an assembly file:

- Click **File / Open**.

- Browse to the training Files and open the assembly named:
I-Bracket Assembly.sldasm

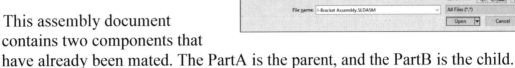

- This assembly document contains two components that have already been mated. The PartA is the parent, and the PartB is the child.

- The goal is to use the geometry of the PartB and create an Offset-Surface that can be used to cut into the PartA, which will become the shape of the final design.

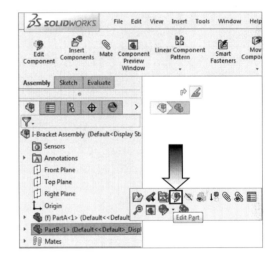

2. Editing the PartB:

- Right click the PartB and select: **Edit Part** (arrow).

- The active part turns blue and the inactive part turns transparent.

- The exploded view is created for clarity only; you do not have to create it.

3. Creating an Offset Surface:

- The Offset Surface command creates a copy of a selected face, or a set of faces. The offset distance can be any value, even zero; and the offset direction can be set to inward or outward.

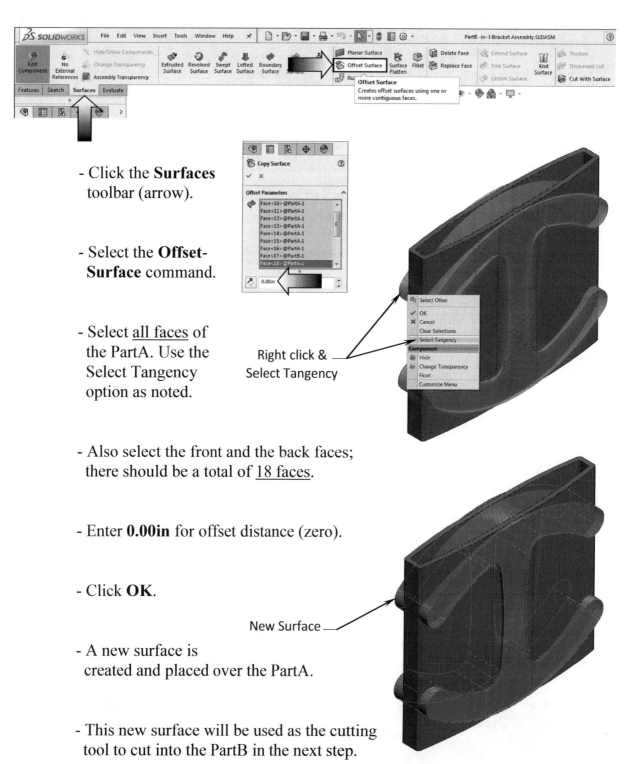

- Click the **Surfaces** toolbar (arrow).

- Select the **Offset-Surface** command.

- Select all faces of the PartA. Use the Select Tangency option as noted.

Right click & Select Tangency

- Also select the front and the back faces; there should be a total of 18 faces.

- Enter **0.00in** for offset distance (zero).

- Click **OK**.

New Surface

- A new surface is created and placed over the PartA.

- This new surface will be used as the cutting tool to cut into the PartB in the next step.

9-4

4. Creating a surface cut:

- The Cut With Surface command removes material of a solid or mutibody parts.
  The direction of the cut can be toggled in or out using the reverse option.

- From the Surfaces toolbar, click the **Cut With Surface** command (arrow).

- Under the Surface Cut Parameters select the **Offset Surface** either from the graphics area or from the feature tree.

- Click the **Flip Cut** button to reverse the direction of the cut.

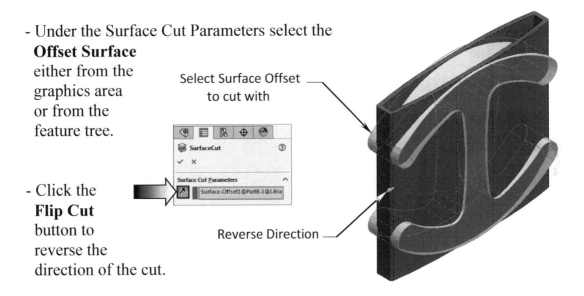

- Verify that the flip cut arrow points outwards. This indicates that all of the material on the outside of the offset surface will be removed, and all that is left will be kept.

- Click **OK**.

- The material on the outside of the PartB is removed, leaving the final shape that looks identical to the PartA.

- The two parts are overlapping one another, we will need to hide one of them.

5. Hiding a component:

- Using the Feature tree right click the PartA and select: **Hide Component** (arrow).

Note: *Hiding a component is simply removing it from the scene, but it still resides in the memory.*

Suppressing a component will not only remove it from the scene, but also from the memory as well.

- The PartA is removed from the graphics, and on the feature tree its icon changes to a white color.

6. Hiding a surface:

- To see the final shape of the PartB, we also need to hide the Surface Offset.

- Using the feature tree once again, expand the component PartB (click the plus sign in front of the name).

- Right click the feature **Surface Offset1** and select **Hide** (arrow).

- The offset surface is removed from the graphics, revealing the final shape of the PartB.

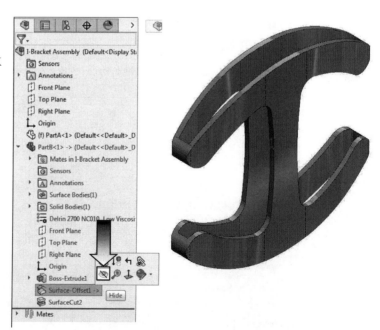

7. Removing the sharp edges:

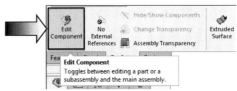

- The PartB needs to have all the sharp edges removed. To do this, a fillet of .090" is added to all of its outer edges.

- The PartB should still be active, if not, right click the PartB and select: **Edit Part**.

- Again, the active part turns blue and the inactive part changes to transparent. The blue color and the amount of transparency can be changed by altering the settings in:
Tools / Options / Colors and Display / Selection.

- Click the **Fillet** command from the Features toolbar.

- Use **Constant Radius** and enter **.090"** for radius size.

- Select all edges on the <u>outside</u> of the part as noted (right click one edge and pick: Select Tangency).

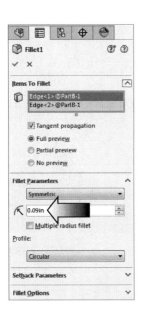 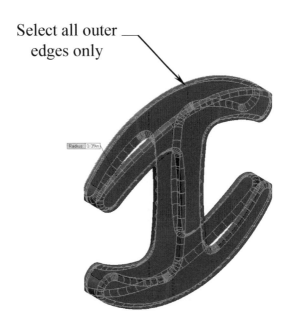

Select all outer edges only

- Click **OK**.

9-7

8. Exiting the Edit Component mode:

- Click off the **Edit Component** button to return to the Edit Assembly mode. The final mass of the part needs to be calculated next.

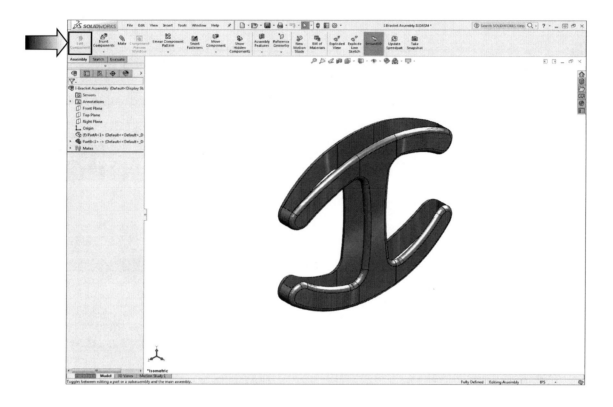

9. Calculating the mass:

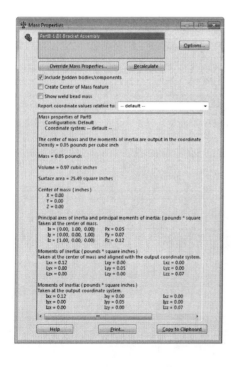

- From the Evaluate tab, click **Mass Properties**.

- Using two decimals, **enter the mass** of the part here:

_____ lbs.

- **Save** and **Close** the assembly document.

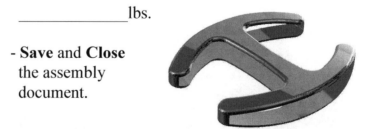

NOTE: Refer to the completed assembly saved in the Training files folder for reference or to compare your results against it.

Exercise: Cut with Surface

1. Opening a part document:

- Click **File / Open**.

- Browse to the Training Files, locate and open the part named: **Cut with Surface 1_of_2 _Exe**.

- This first part is a <u>surface model</u>, created and saved as a different format, therefore no feature history is available.

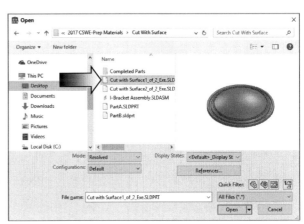

2. Inserting a part document:

- Click **Insert / Part**.

- Browse to the training Files, locate and open the part document named: **Cut with Surface 2_of_2 _Exe**.

- This second part document is a <u>solid model</u>, also created and saved as a different file format; there is no history available for editing.

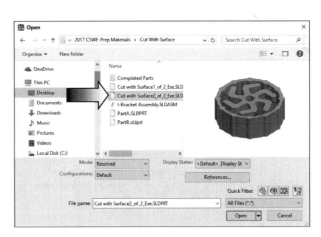

- The two parts will be placed on top of one another, and the surface model will be used as the cutting tool to cut into the solid model, and the final designed shape can then be revealed.

- The **Insert Part** dialog box appears on the Properties tree.

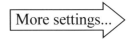

More settings...

- Enable both of the checkboxes:

    * **Locate Part with Move/Copy Feature**.
    * **Break Link to Original Part**.

Click OK to place the part on Origin

- Click **OK**. The **Locate Part** dialog box appears.

- Click **OK** again to place the part on the Origin.

3. Creating a Cut with Surface:

- Switch to the **Surfaces** tool tab.

- Click the **Cut with Surface** command.

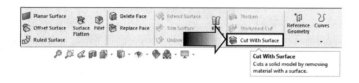

- A surface can be used to cut a solid model. When working with multibody parts, you can select which bodies to keep using the options in the Feature scope.

- The **Surface Cut** dialog appears on the Properties tree.

- For Surface Cut Parameters (cutting tool), select the large revolved surface.

- The cut direction arrow should be pointing downward, if not, click the Reverse direction button (arrow).

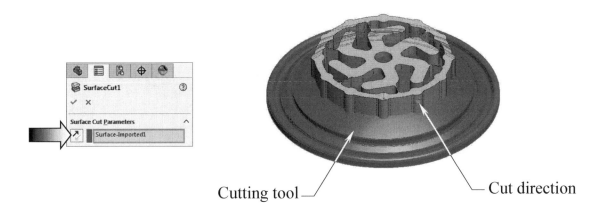

Cutting tool   Cut direction

- Click **OK** to exit the Surface Cut command.

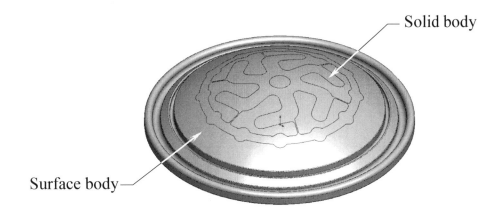

Solid body

Surface body

- The intersection between the two bodies are kept, and the rest of the solid body is removed.

- This cut is similar to the Combine-Common when working with multi-solid-bodies, where multiple bodies are overlapping each other and all materials are removed except that which overlaps.

- The Cutting surface is still visible after the cut. It needs to be hidden so that the final shape can be revealed.

4. Hiding the Cut Surface:

- Click the surface that was used to create the cut in the last step and select the **Hide** command from the pop-up menu.

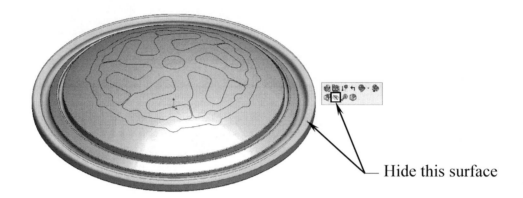

Hide this surface

- Assign **Brass** material to the part.

- Locate the mass of the part and enter it here: _____ lbs.

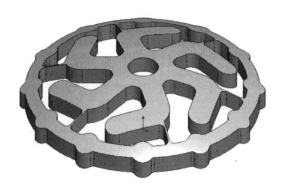

5. Saving your work:

- Click **File / Save As**.

- Enter **Cut with Surface_Exe** for the name of the file.

- Press **Save** and then close all documents.

CHAPTER 10

Creating a Curved Spring

CSWE Exam Preparation
Creating a Curved Spring

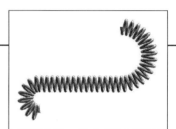

A swept feature is created by moving a profile along a path. The profile should be closed to create a solid feature, and if the profile is open, a thin or a surface feature can be made from it.

The path may be opened or closed and can be created from a set of sketched curves, a group of model edges or one continuous sketch entity.

The profile is sketched on a plane that is normal to the path, and is coincident or pierced to the path. When the profile is moved along the path the twisting effects can be created or minimized, but must not be intersected with itself.

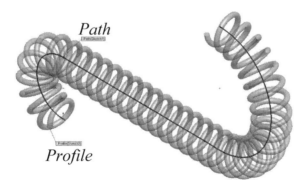

Path

Profile

Depending on the requirements and the level of accuracy of the design, there are several approaches for creating a swept feature. This chapter discusses a method that helps control the twisting of the sweep where a small circle, which is the wire diameter of the spring, will be used as the sweep profile; and the path will start out as a sketch and get twisted into a helix. The twist type is set to Turns, and the number of turns is defined, then the profile is moved and twisted along the path based on the information entered.

CSWE Exam Preparation
Creating a Curved Spring

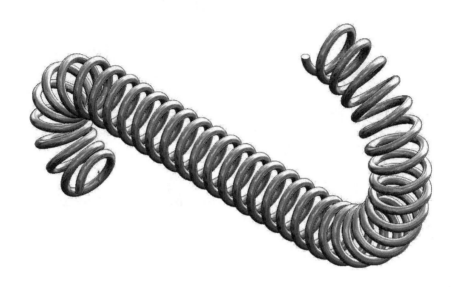

Dimensioning Standards: **ANSI**

Units: **INCHES** – 3 Decimals

Tools Needed:

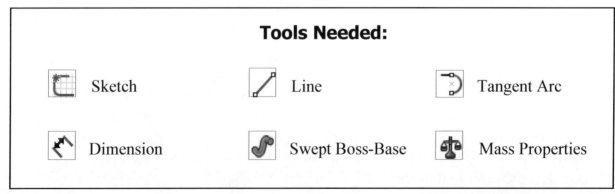

1. Starting a new part:

- Click **File / New**.

- Select the **Part** template and click **OK**.

- Change the units to **IPS** and Drafting Standards to **ANSI**.

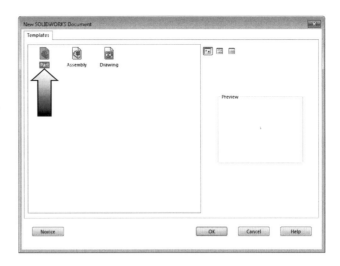

2. Creating the sweep path:

- Select the Front plane and open a new sketch.

- Sketch the profile shown below using the line and tangent arc commands. Notice the location of the origin? It should be at the bottom end of the smaller arc.

- Add the dimensions and relations as noted to fully define the sketch.

- Exit the sketch.

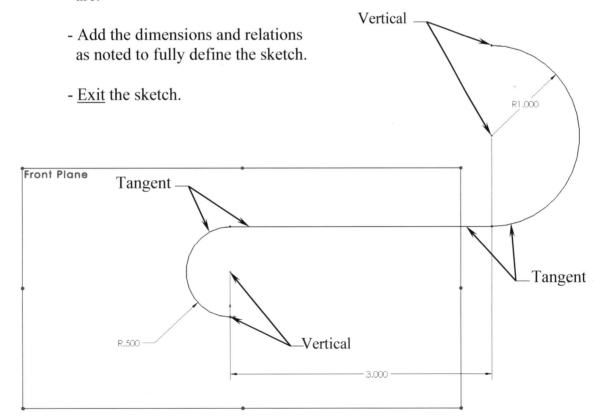

- A sweep feature requires two sketches, one profile and one path. The first sketch is the path, and the second sketch is the profile. We will sketch the profile next.

10-3

3. Creating the sweep profile:

- Select the Top plane and open a new sketch.

- Sketch a **Circle** slightly away from the origin.

- Add the dimensions and a vertical relation as shown.

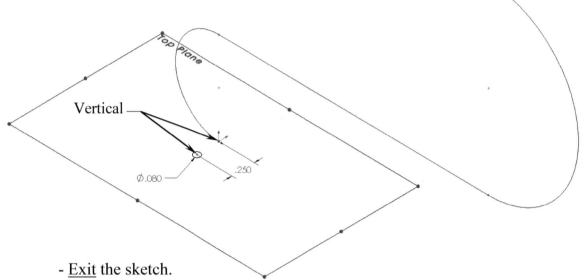

- Exit the sketch.

4. Creating a swept feature:

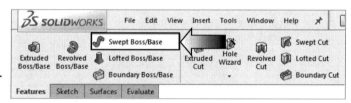

- Switch to the Features toolbar and select the **Swept Boss/Base** command.

- Select the **second sketch** (the small circle) for Sweep Profile.

- Select the **first sketch** for Sweep Path (click one of the entities).

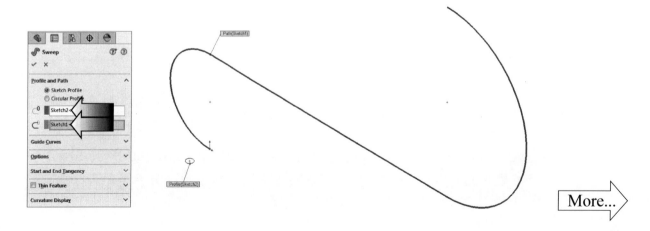

More...

10-4

- Expand the **Options** section and select the following:

   * Orientation/Twist Type: **Twist Along Path**
   * Define By: **Turns**
   * Number of Turns: **40**

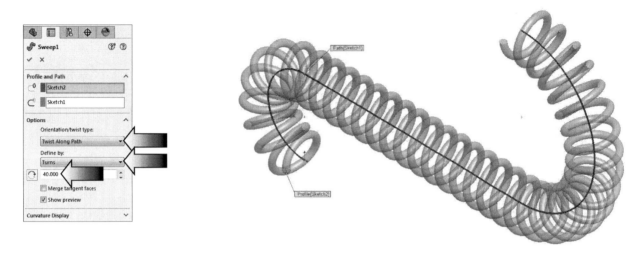

- Click **OK**.

5. Assigning material:

- From the FeatureManager tree, right click the Material selection and select **Edit Material**.

- Expand the Steel folder, select **Alloy Steel** from the list, and click: **Apply / Close**.

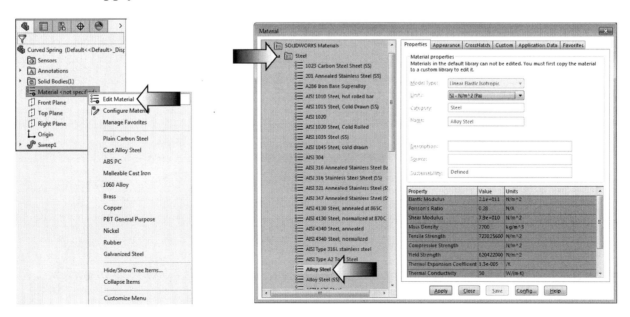

6. Calculating the mass:

- After the material has been specified, the information from the model such as Mass, Center of Mass, Surface Area, and Volume can be retrieved from the Evaluation tool tab.

- Switch to the Evaluation tab and click the Mass Properties command, or select the menus **Tools / Mass Properties**.

- If needed, click the **Options** button and change the settings to **Use Custom Settings** to Inches, and three Decimal Places.

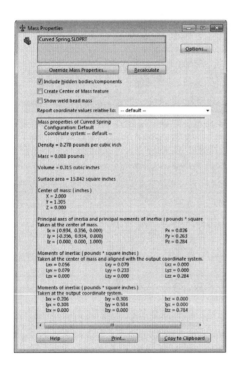

- Using three decimals, **enter the mass here:**

_____ lbs.

7. Saving your work:

- Click **File / Save As**.

- Enter **Curved Spring** for the file name.

- Press **Save**.

NOTE: Refer to the completed part saved in the Training Files folder for reference, or to compare your results against it.

Exercise: Circular Spring

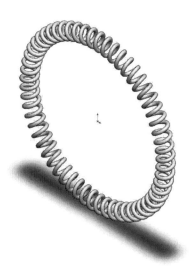

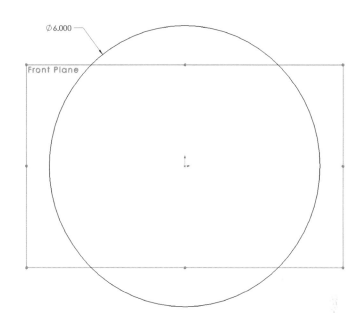

1. Sketching the Sweep Path:

- Select the <u>Front</u> plane and open a new sketch.

- Sketch a Circle as shown and add a diameter dimension to fully define the sketch.

- **Exit** the sketch.

2. Sketching the Sweep Profile:

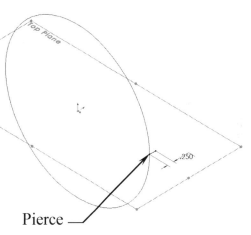

- Select the <u>Top</u> plane and open a new sketch.

- Sketch a Horizontal line towards the right.

- Add a Pierce relation and a **.250 in**. dimension.

- **Exit** the sketch.

3. Creating a Swept <u>Surface</u>:

- Click 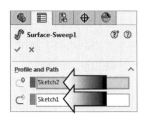 or select **Insert / Surface / Sweep**.

- Select the **Horizontal-Line** for use as the Sweep Profile.

- Select the **Circle** as the Sweep Path.

10-7

- Expand the **Options** dialog box.

- Select **Twist Along Path**, under the Orientation / Twist Type.

- For Define By: Select **Turns**.

- For number of Turns: Enter **60**.

- Click **OK**.

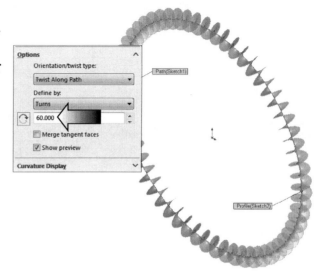

4. Sketching the Wire-Diameter:

- Select the Front plane and open a new sketch.

- Sketch a **Circle** on the right side of the swept surface.

- Add a Pierce relation and a **Ø.125 in**. diameter dimension.

- **Exit** the sketch.

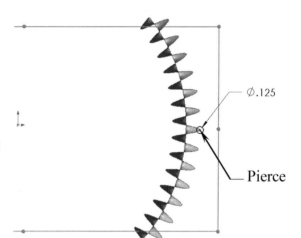

5. Creating a Swept Boss-Base: (Solid)

- Click [icon] or select **Insert / Bose-Base / Sweep**.

- Select the **Circle** for use as the Sweep Profile.

- For Sweep Path, select the **Edge** of the Swept-Surface.

- Click **OK**.

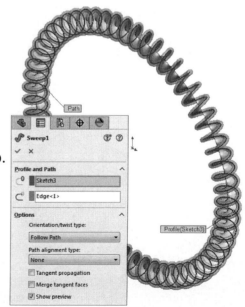

6. Hiding the Swept-Surface:

- Right click on the Swept-Surface and select **Hide** 👁.

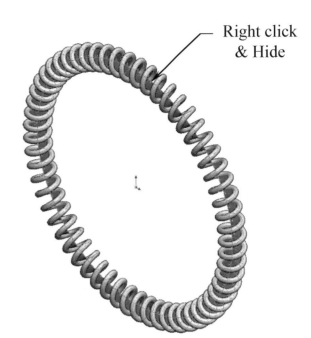

Right click & Hide

7. Saving your work:

- Select **File / Save As.**

- For file name, enter: **Circular Spring**.

- Click **Save**.

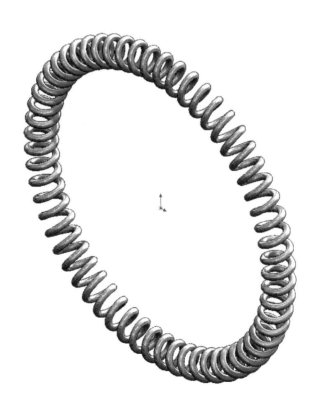

Spring Examples

Flat Spring

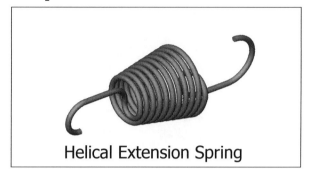
Helical Extension Spring

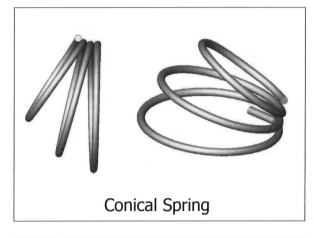
Conical Spring

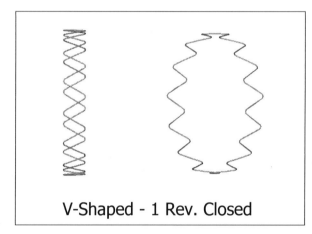
V-Shaped - 1 Rev. Closed

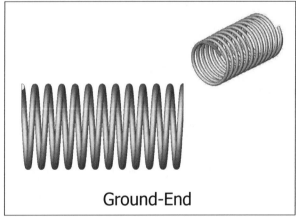
Ground-End

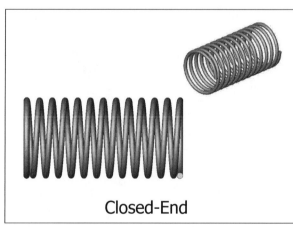
Closed-End

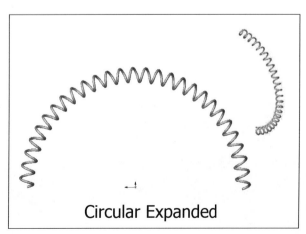
Circular Expanded

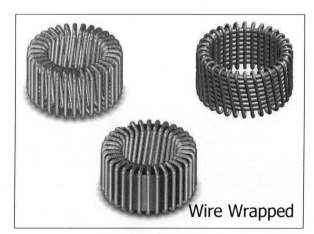
Wire Wrapped

Chapter 11

Surface Modifications

CSWE Exam Preparation
Surface Modifications

When working with imported parts, whether the imported model is a solid model or a surface model, we will have to deal with one major disadvantage, and that is not having the features history available for modifications.

The SOLIDWORKS software offers a few tools for manipulating the geometry of the imported model such as surface move, rotate, copy, delete, etc. When used together with the surfaces commands, much more can be achieved.

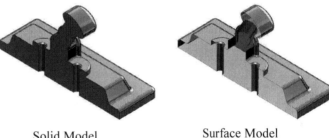

Solid Model   Surface Model

When a surface model has a number of faces that consists of a closed volume, it can be converted into a solid model. However, if the surface model is opened, it can only be made into a thin walled part.

 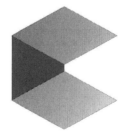

Closed Volume = Solid Model   Opened = Surface Model

This lesson focuses on the techniques that are used in the CSWE exam, where the solid model will be converted into a surface model, and the handle will be rotated into the upright position. The deleted faces will be patched up and knitted to the entire model and then become one closed volume. The volume will then get converted back to a solid model.

CSWE Exam Preparation
Surface Modifications

Dimensioning Standards: **ANSI**

Units: **INCHES** – 3 Decimals

Tools Needed:

Temporary Axis		Move / Copy		Delete Surface	
Loft Surface		Trim Surface		Knit Surface	

CSWE 2017 | Exam Preparation | Surface Modifications

1. Opening a part document:

- Click **File / Open**.

- Browse to the Training Files folder and open the part document named: **Steel Handle**.

- This model was created as a solid, but the approach that we are about to take will convert it to a surface model.

- The sample images below show the cross sections of the model, before and after the Delete Face operation.

2. Deleting the faces of the model:

- Right click on one of the two faces as indicated below and select the **Delete** option below the Face selection.

- The Delete Face options appear on the Properties tree.

Solid model

- Click the **Delete** option and select the two faces as noted.

- Click **OK**. The two selected faces are removed and the Solid model is changed to a Surface model.

Surface model

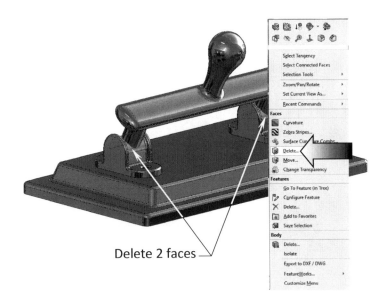

Delete 2 faces

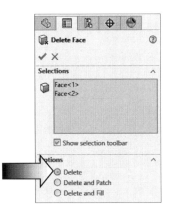

- Rotate and zoom closer to examine the result.

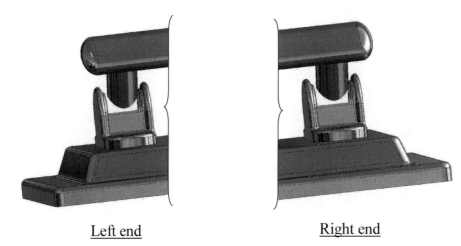

Left end   Right end

- The model has been converted into a surface model, there is no mass in it, and the Mass Properties command is grayed out at the moment.

- The intention is to separate the handle from the base, so that it can be rotated to the upright position. The two deleted faces will get recreated and knitted to form a closed volume and then thicken into a solid.

3. Measuring the current angle:

- Change to the Right orientation (Control + 4), and enable the **Temporary-Axis** from the **View** pull down menu.

- Switch to the **Evaluate** tool tab and select the **Measure** command.

- Measure the angle between the **Right** plane and the center **axis** of the handle.

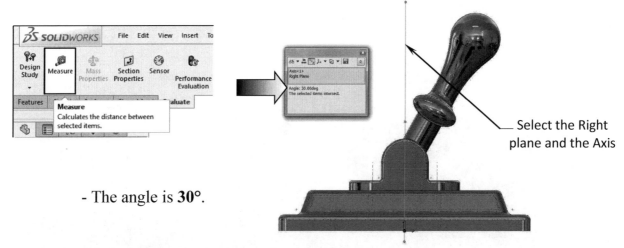

- The angle is **30°**.

- Exit the Measure command.

4. Rotating the handle:

- Select the **Move/Copy** command (arrow) from the **Insert / Features** pull down menu.

- At the bottom of the Properties tree, click the **Translate/Rotate** button (arrow).

- Under the Bodies to Move / Copy selection box, select the Handle from the Surface Bodies folder (arrow).

- Expand the Rotate selection box and select the Axis as indicated below.

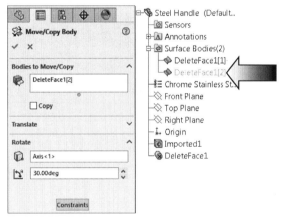

- Enter **30deg** for angle.

- Click **OK**.

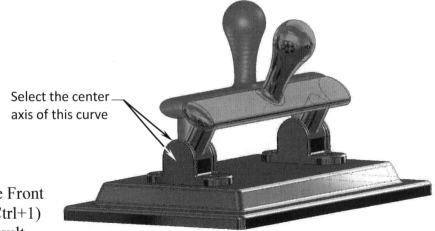

Select the center axis of this curve

- Change to the Front orientation (Ctrl+1) to view the result.

5. Recreating the deleted surfaces:

- Now that the handle is rotated to the upright position, we can fill the gaps between the handle and the base. One of the commands to do that is the Surface Loft command.

- Switch to the **Surfaces** tool tab and select the **Lofted Surface** command.

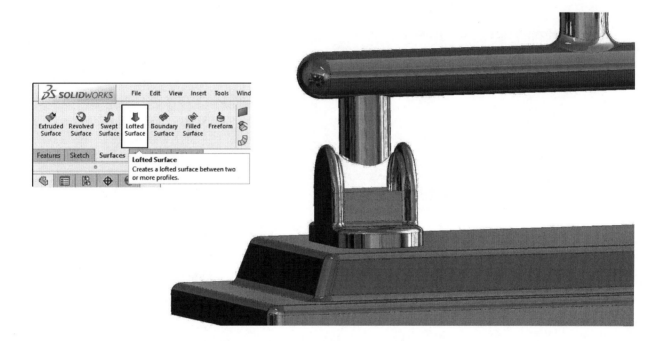

- Under the **Profile** selection box, select the two curve edges as indicated below (more settings on next page).

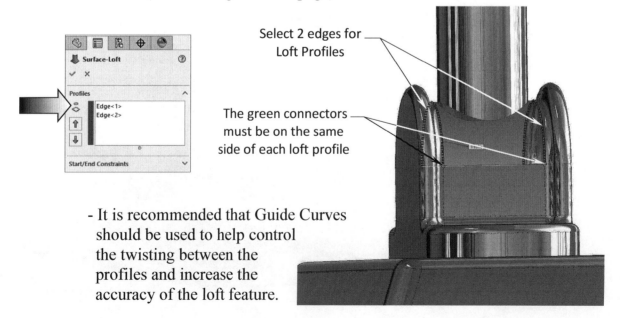

Select 2 edges for Loft Profiles

The green connectors must be on the same side of each loft profile

- It is recommended that Guide Curves should be used to help control the twisting between the profiles and increase the accuracy of the loft feature.

- Click inside the **Guide Curves** selection box to activate this option.

- Select the <u>two linear edges</u> on both sides as noted, to use as guide curves.

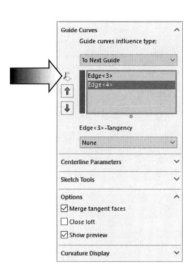

Select 2 edges for Guide Curves

- Under the **Options** selection box, enable the checkbox **Merge Tangent Faces**.

- Also enable the **Show Preview** checkbox.

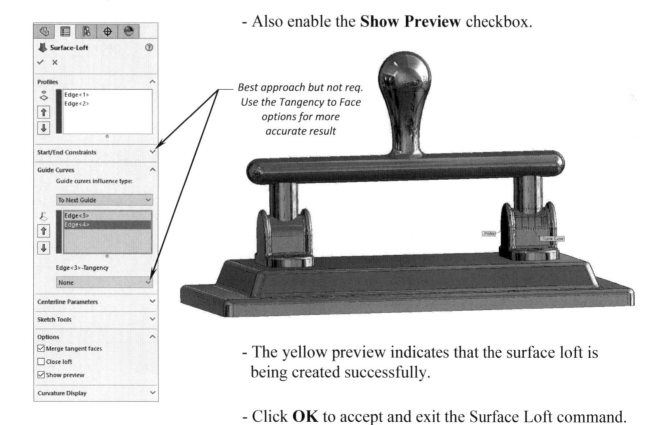

Best approach but not req. Use the Tangency to Face options for more accurate result

- The yellow preview indicates that the surface loft is being created successfully.

- Click **OK** to accept and exit the Surface Loft command.

- Repeat step 5 and create another Lofted-Surface to fill the opening on the other end of the handle.

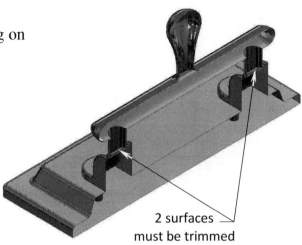

2 surfaces must be trimmed

- Create a section view using the Right plane. Verify that all gaps have been filled at this point.

- There are two surfaces under the handle that need to be trimmed, and it is quite difficult to see clearly where they are. So we are going to hide the base and only work with the handle.

6. Hiding a surface body:

- One of the major advantages in working with multibody parts is the ability to hide or show any of the bodies at any time, and a new feature can be added to the selected body without affecting the others.

- The bodies can be selected directly from the graphics area or from the Surface Bodies folder, listed on the FeatureManager tree.

- Click anywhere on the base and select the **Hide** command (arrow).

7. Trimming surfaces:

- Rotate the view and locate the two surfaces under the handle as noted.

- Click the **Trim Surface** command from the Surfaces tool tab.

- Under the **Trim Type** selection box, click the **Mutual** option.

- Under **Trimming-Surfaces**, select the two trim surfaces and the Handle.

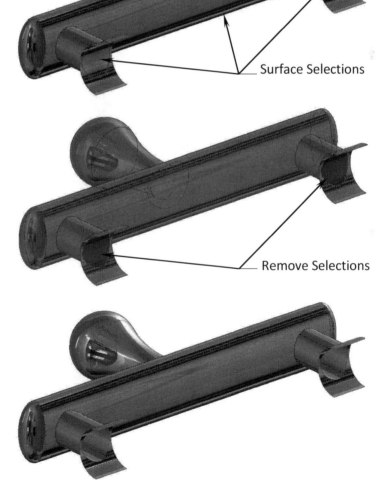

Surface Selections

Remove Selections

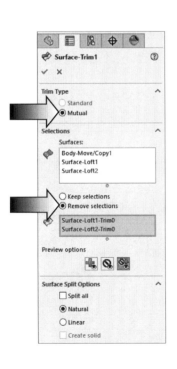

- Click the **Remove-Selections** option and select the two faces again.

- Click **OK** to exit the Trim Surface.

8. Showing a surface body:

- After the trim we need to make the base body visible for the next step.

- Right click the Base body (DeleteFace1) and select **Show**.

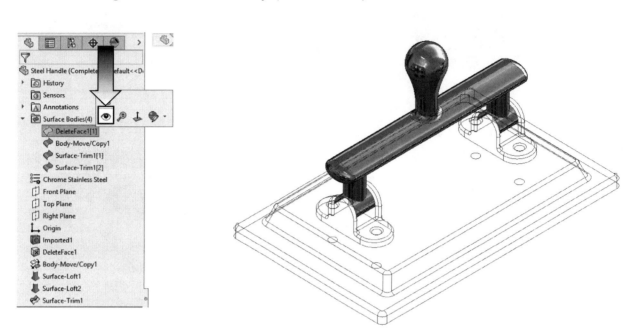

- The base body appears. We can now knit the base body to the other surface bodies, so that they can become one closed volume.

9. Knitting all surface bodies:

- Click the **Knit Surface** command from the Surfaces tool tab.

- Select <u>all surface bodies</u> either from the graphics area or from the Feature tree.

- Enable the **Try To Form Solid** checkbox.

- Click **OK**.

- The surface model is converted back to a solid model.

10. Creating a section view:

- Select the **Right** plane from the FeatureManager tree.

- Click the **Section View** command on the View Heads Up toolbar.

- Verify that the part is now a solid model.

- Click **Cancel** to exit the section view command.

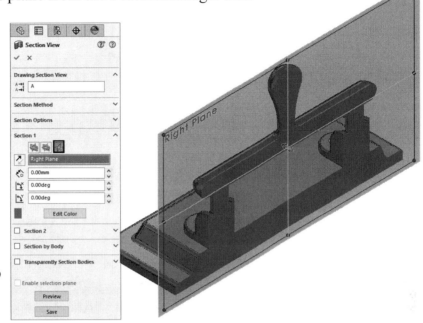

11. Measuring the mass:

- Change the material to **Chrome Stainless Steel**.

- Click the **Mass Properties** command from the Evaluate tool tab.

- Using three decimal places **enter the final mass** of the model here: _____ lbs.

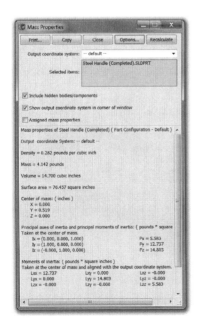

- Save the document as **Surface Modifications Completed** and close all documents.

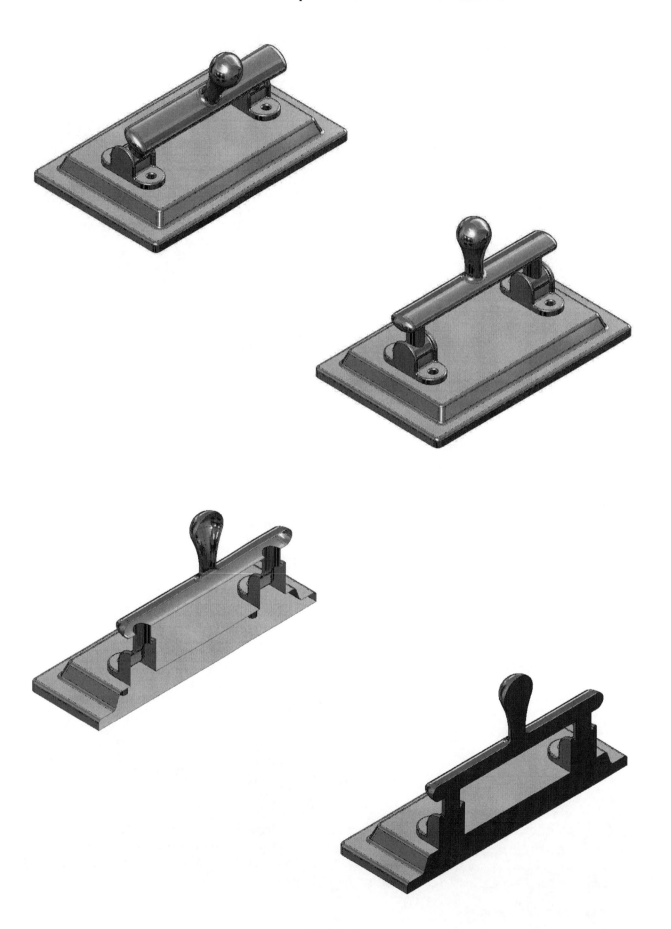

Glossary

Alloys:

An Alloy is a mixture of two or more metals (and sometimes a non-metal). The mixture is made by heating and melting the substances together.
Example of alloys are Bronze (Copper and Tin), Brass (Copper and Zinc), and Steel (Iron and Carbon).

Gravity and Mass:

Gravity is the force that pulls everything on earth toward the ground and makes things feel heavy. Gravity makes all falling bodies accelerate at a constant 32ft. per second (9.8 m/s). In the earth's atmosphere, air resistance slows acceleration. Only on airless Moon would a feather and a metal block fall to the ground together.
The mass of an object is the amount of material it contains.
A body with greater mass has more inertia; it needs a greater force to accelerate.
Weight depends on the force of gravity, but mass does not.

When an object spins around another (for example: a satellite orbiting the earth) it is pushed outward. Two forces are at work here: Centrifugal (pushing outward) and Centripetal (pulling inward). If you whirl a ball around you on a string, you pull it inward (Centripetal force). The ball seems to pull outward (Centrifugal force) and if released will fly off in a straight line.

Heat:

Heat is a form of energy and can move from one substance to another in one of three ways: by Convection, by Radiation, and by Conduction.

- Convection takes place only in liquids like water (for example: water in a kettle) and gases (for example: air warmed by a heat source such as a fire or radiator). When liquid or gas is heated, it expands and becomes less dense. Warm air above the radiator rises and cool air moves in to take its place, creating a convection current.

- Radiation is movement of heat through the air. Heat forms match set molecules of air moving and rays of heat spread out around the heat source.

- Conduction occurs in solids such as metals. The handle of a metal spoon left in boiling liquid warms up as molecules at the heated end moves faster and collide with their neighbors, setting them moving. The heat travels through the metal, which is a good conductor of heat.

Inertia:

A body with a large mass is harder to start and also to stop. A heavy truck traveling at 50mph needs more power breaks to stop its motion than a smaller car traveling at the same speed.
Inertia is the tendency of an object either to stay still or to move steadily in a straight line, unless another force (such as a brick wall stopping the vehicle) makes it behave differently.

Joules:

The Joules are the SI unit of work or energy.
One Joule of work is done when a force of one Newton moves a distance of one meter.
The Joule is named after the English scientist James Joule (1818-1889).

Materials:

- Stainless steel is an alloy of steel with chromium or nickel.

- Steel is made by the basic oxygen process. The raw material is about three parts melted iron and one part scrap steel. Blowing oxygen into the melted iron raises the temperature and gets rid of impurities.

- All plastics are chemical compounds called polymers.

- Glass is made by mixing and heating sand, limestone, and soda ash. When these ingredients melt they turn into glass, which is hardened when it cools. Glass is in fact not a solid but a "supercooled" liquid, it can be shaped by blowing, pressing, drawing, casting into molds, rolling, and floating across molten tin, to make large sheets.

- Ceramic objects, such as pottery and porcelain, electrical insulators, bricks, and roof tiles are all made from clay. The clay is shaped or molded when wet and soft, and heated in a kiln until it hardens.

Machine Tools:

Are powered tools used for shaping metal or other materials, by drilling holes, chiseling, grinding, pressing or cutting. Often the material (the work piece) is moved while the tool stays still (lathe), or vice versa, the work piece stayed while the tool moves (mill).
Most common machine tools are: Mill, Lathe, Saw, Broach, Punch press, Grind, Bore and Stamp break.

CNC

Computer Numerical Control is the automation of machine tools that are operated by precisely programmed commands encoded on a storage medium, as opposed to controlled manually via hand wheels or levers, or mechanically automated via cams alone. Most CNC today is computer numerical control in which computers play an integral part of the control.

3D Printing

All methods work by working in layers, adding material, etc. different to other techniques, which are subtractive. Support is needed because almost all methods could support multi material printing, but it is currently only available in certain top tier machines.

A method of turning digital shapes into physical objects. Due to its nature, it allows us to accurately control the shape of the product. The drawback is size restraints and materials are often not durable.

While FDM doesn't seem like the best method for instrument manufacturing, it is one of the cheapest and most universally available methods.

EDM
Electric Discharge Machining.

FDM
Fused Deposition Modeling.

SLA
Stereo Lithography.

SLS
Selective Laser Sintering.

SLM
Selective Laser Melting.

J-P
Jetted Photopolymer (or Polyjet)

EDM Electric Discharge Machining

The basic EDM process is really quite simple. An electrical spark is created between an electrode and a work piece. The spark is visible evidence of the flow of electricity. This electric spark produces intense heat with temperatures reaching 8000 to 12000 degrees Celsius, melting almost anything.

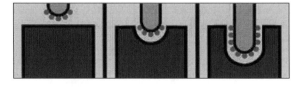

The spark is very carefully controlled and localized so that it only affects the surface of the material.

The EDM process usually does not effect the heat treat below the surface. With wire EDM the spark always takes place in the dielectric of deionized water. The conductivity of the water is carefully controlled making an excellent environment for the EDM process. The water acts as a coolant and flushes away the eroded metal particles.

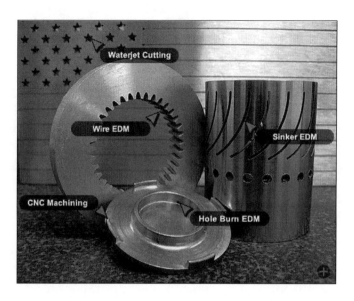

FDM Fused Deposition Modeling

3D printers that run on FDM Technology build parts layer-by-layer by heating thermoplastic material to a semi-liquid state and extruding it according to computer controlled paths.

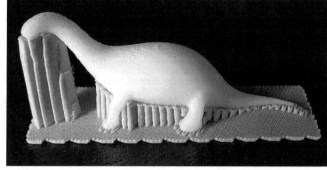

FDM uses two materials to execute a print job: modeling material, which constitutes the finished piece, and support material, which acts as scaffolding. Material filaments are fed from the 3D printer's material bays to the print head, which moves in X and Y coordinates, depositing material to complete each layer before the base moves down the Z axis and the next layer begins.

Once the 3D printer is done building, the user breaks the support material away or dissolves it in detergent and water, and the part is ready to use.

SLA StereoLithograph Apparatus

Stereolithography is an additive fabrication process utilizing a vat of liquid UV-curable photopolymer "resin" and a UV laser to build parts a layer at a time. On each

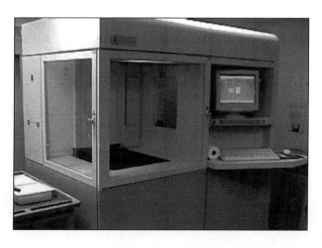

layer, the laser beam traces a part cross-section pattern on the surface of the liquid resin. Exposure to the UV laser light cures, or, solidifies the pattern traced on the resin and adheres it to the layer below.

After a pattern has been traced, the SLA's elevator platform descends by a single layer thickness, typically .0019in to .0059in. Then, a resin-filled blade sweeps across the part cross section, re-coating it with fresh material. On this new liquid surface the subsequent layer pattern is traced, adhering to the previous layer.

A complcte 3-D part is formed by this process. After building, parts are cleaned of excess resin by immersion in a chemical bath and then cured in a UV oven.

SLS Selective Laser Sintering

Selective laser sintering (SLS) is an additive manufacturing (AM) technique that uses a laser as the power source to sinter (compacting) metal), aiming the laser automatically at points in space defined by a 3D model, binding the material together to create a solid structure.

It is similar to direct metal laser sintering (DMLS); the two are instantiations of the same concept but differ in technical details.
Selective laser melting (SLM) uses a comparable concept, but in SLM the material is fully melted rather than sintered,[1] allowing different properties (crystal structure, porosity, and so on). SLS (as well as the other mentioned AM techniques) is a relatively new technology that so far has mainly been used for rapid prototyping and for low-volume production of component parts. Production roles are expanding as the commercialization of AM technology improves.

SLM Selective Laser Melting

Selective laser melting is an additive manufacturing process that uses 3D CAD data as a digital information source and energy in the form of a high-power laser beam, to create three-dimensional metal parts by fusing fine metal powders together. Manufacturing applications in

aerospace or medical orthopedics are being pioneered.

The process starts by slicing the 3D CAD file data into layers, usually from 20 to 100 micrometres thick (0.00078740157 to 0.00393700787 in) creating a 2D image of each layer; this file format is the industry standard .stl file used on most layer-based 3D printing or stereolithography technologies.

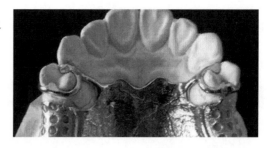

This file is then loaded into a file preparation software package that assigns parameters, values and physical supports that allow the file to be interpreted and built by different types of additive manufacturing machines.

J-P Jetted Photopolymer (or Polyjet)

Photopolymer jetting (or PolyJet) builds prototypes by jetting liquid photopolymer resin from ink-jet style heads. The resin is sprayed from the moving heads, and only the amount of material needed is used.

UV light is simultaneously emitted from the head, which cures each layer of resin immediately after it is applied. The process produces excellent surface finish and feature detail. Photopolymer jetting is used primarily to check form and fit, and can handle limited functional tests due to the limited strength of photopolymer resins.

This process offers the unique ability to create prototypes with more than one type of material. For instance a toothbrush prototype could be composed with a rigid shaft with a rubber-like over-molding for grip.

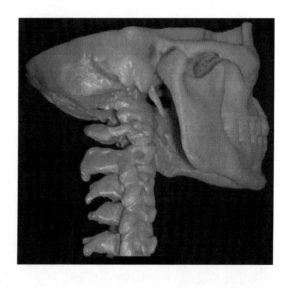

The process works with a variety of proprietary photopolymer resins as opposed to production materials. A tradeoff with this technology is that exposure to ambient heat, humidity or sunlight can cause dimensional change that can effect tolerance. The process is faster and cleaner than the traditional vat and laser photo-polymer processes.

Carbon 3D

The Carbon 3D not only prints composite Materials like carbon fiber, but also fiberglass, nylon and PLA. Of course, only one at a time.

The printer employs some pretty nifty advancements, including a self-leveling printing bed that clicks into position before each print.

The Carbon 3D is groundbreaking 3D printing technology which is 25 to 100 times faster than currently available commercial PolyJet or SLA machines.

It is a true quantum leap forward for 3D printing speed!

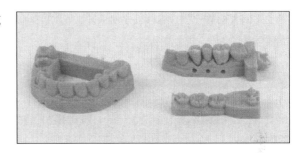

Newton's Law:

1. Every object remains stopped or goes on moving at a steady rate in a straight line unless acted upon by another force. This is the inertia principle.
2. The amount of force needed to make an object change its speed depends on the mass of the object and the amount of the acceleration or deceleration required.
3. To every action there is an equal and opposite reaction. When a body is pushed on its way by a force, another force pushes back with equal strength.

Polymers:
A polymer is made of one or more large molecules formed from thousands of smaller molecules. Rubber and Wood are natural polymers. Plastics are synthetic (artificially made) polymers.

Speed and Velocity:

- Speed is the rate at which a moving object changes position (how far it moves in a fixed time).
- Velocity is speed in a particular direction.
- If either speed or direction is changed, velocity also changed.

Absorbed
A feature, sketch, or annotation that is contained in another item (usually a feature) in the FeatureManager design tree. Examples are the profile sketch and profile path in a base-sweep, or a cosmetic thread annotation in a hole.

Align
Tools that assist in lining up annotations and dimensions (left, right, top, bottom, and so on). For aligning parts in an assembly.

Alternate position view
A drawing view in which one or more views are superimposed in phantom lines on the original view. Alternate position views are often used to show the range of motion of an assembly.

Anchor point
The end of a leader that attaches to the note, block, or other annotation. Sheet formats contain anchor points for a bill of materials, a hole table, a revision table, and a weldment cut list.

Annotation
A text note or a symbol that adds specific design intent to a part, assembly, or drawing. Specific types of annotations include note, hole callout, surface finish symbol, datum feature symbol, datum target, geometric tolerance symbol, weld symbol, balloon, and stacked balloon. Annotations that apply only to drawings include center mark, annotation centerline, area hatch, and block.

Appearance callouts
Callouts that display the colors and textures of the face, feature, body, and part under the entity selected and are a shortcut to editing colors and textures.

Area hatch
A crosshatch pattern or fill applied to a selected face or to a closed sketch in a drawing.

Assembly
A document in which parts, features, and other assemblies (sub-assemblies) are mated together. The parts and sub-assemblies exist in documents separate from the assembly. For example, in an assembly, a piston can be mated to other parts, such as a connecting rod or cylinder. This new assembly can then be used as a sub-assembly in an assembly of an engine. The extension for a SOLIDWORKS assembly file name is .SLDASM.

Attachment point
The end of a leader that attaches to the model (to an edge, vertex, or face, for example) or to a drawing sheet.

Axis
A straight line that can be used to create model geometry, features, or patterns. An axis can be made in a number of different ways, including using the intersection of two planes.

Balloon
Labels parts in an assembly, typically including item numbers and quantity. In drawings, the item numbers are related to rows in a bill of materials.

Base
The first solid feature of a part.

Baseline dimensions
Sets of dimensions measured from the same edge or vertex in a drawing.

Bend
A feature in a sheet metal part. A bend generated from a filleted corner, cylindrical face, or conical face is a round bend; a bend generated from sketched straight lines is a sharp bend.

Bill of materials
A table inserted into a drawing to keep a record of the parts used in an assembly.

Block
A user-defined annotation that you can use in parts, assemblies, and drawings. A block can contain text, sketch entities (except points), and area hatch, and it can be saved in a file for later use as, for example, a custom callout or a company logo.

Bottom-up assembly
An assembly modeling technique where you create parts and then insert them into an assembly.

Broken-out section
A drawing view that exposes inner details of a drawing view by removing material from a closed profile, usually a spline.

Cavity
The mold half that holds the cavity feature of the design part.

Center mark
A cross that marks the center of a circle or arc.

Centerline
A centerline marks, in phantom font, an axis of symmetry in a sketch or drawing.

Chamfer
Bevels a selected edge or vertex. You can apply chamfers to both sketches and features.

Child
A dependent feature related to a previously-built feature. For example, a chamfer on the edge of a hole is a child of the parent hole.

Click-release
As you sketch, if you click and then release the pointer, you are in click-release mode. Move the pointer and click again to define the next point in the sketch sequence.

Click-drag
As you sketch, if you click and drag the pointer, you are in click-drag mode. When you release the pointer, the sketch entity is complete.

Closed profile
Also called a closed contour, it is a sketch or sketch entity with no exposed endpoints; for example, a circle or polygon.

Collapse
The opposite of explode. The collapse action returns an exploded assembly's parts to their normal positions.

Collision Detection
An assembly function that detects collisions between components when components move or rotate. A collision occurs when an entity on one component coincides with any entity on another component.

Component
Any part or sub-assembly within an assembly

Configuration
A variation of a part or assembly within a single document. Variations can include different dimensions, features, and properties. For example, a single part such as a bolt can contain different configurations that vary the diameter and length.

ConfigurationManager
Located on the left side of the SOLIDWORKS window, it is a means to create, select, and view the configurations of parts and assemblies.

Constraint
The relations between sketch entities, or between sketch entities and planes, axes, edges, or vertices.

Construction geometry
The characteristic of a sketch entity that the entity is used in creating other geometry but is not itself used in creating features.

Coordinate system
A system of planes used to assign Cartesian coordinates to features, parts, and assemblies. Part and assembly documents contain default coordinate systems; other coordinate systems can be defined with reference geometry. Coordinate systems can be used with measurement tools and for exporting documents to other file formats.

Cosmetic thread
An annotation that represents threads.

Crosshatch
A pattern (or fill) applied to drawing views such as section views and broken-out sections.

Curvature
Curvature is equal to the inverse of the radius of the curve. The curvature can be displayed in different colors according to the local radius (usually of a surface).

Cut
A feature that removes material from a part by such actions as extrude, revolve, loft, sweep, thicken, cavity, and so on.

Dangling
A dimension, relation, or drawing section view that is unresolved. For example, if a piece of geometry is dimensioned, and that geometry is later deleted, the dimension becomes dangling.

Degrees of freedom
Geometry that is not defined by dimensions or relations is free to move. In 2D sketches, there are three degrees of freedom: movement along the X and Y axes, and rotation about the Z axis (the axis normal to the sketch plane). In 3D sketches and in assemblies, there are six degrees of freedom: movement along the X, Y, and Z axes, and rotation about the X, Y, and Z axes.

Derived part
A derived part is a new base, mirror, or component part created directly from an existing part and linked to the original part such that changes to the original part are reflected in the derived part.

Derived sketch
A copy of a sketch, in either the same part or the same assembly that is connected to the original sketch. Changes in the original sketch are reflected in the derived sketch.

Design Library
Located in the Task Pane, the Design Library provides a central location for reusable elements such as parts, assemblies, and so on.

Design table
An Excel spreadsheet that is used to create multiple configurations in a part or assembly document.

Detached drawing
A drawing format that allows opening and working in a drawing without loading the corresponding models into memory. The models are loaded on an as-needed basis.

Detail view
A portion of a larger view, usually at a larger scale than the original view.

Dimension line
A linear dimension line references the dimension text to extension lines indicating the entity being measured. An angular dimension line references the dimension text directly to the measured object.

DimXpertManager
Located on the left side of the SOLIDWORKS window, it is a means to manage dimensions and tolerances created using DimXpert for parts according to the requirements of the ASME Y.14.41-2003 standard.

DisplayManager
The DisplayManager lists the appearances, decals, lights, scene, and cameras applied to the current model. From the DisplayManager, you can view applied content, and add, edit, or delete items. When PhotoView 360 is added in, the DisplayManager also provides access to PhotoView options.

Document
A file containing a part, assembly, or drawing.

Draft
The degree of taper or angle of a face, usually applied to molds or castings.

Drawing
A 2D representation of a 3D part or assembly. The extension for a SOLIDWORKS drawing file name is .SLDDRW.

Drawing sheet
A page in a drawing document.

Driven dimension
Measurements of the model, but they do not drive the model and their values cannot be changed.

Driving dimension
Also referred to as a model dimension, it sets the value for a sketch entity. It can also control distance, thickness, and feature parameters.

Edge
A single outside boundary of a feature.

Edge flange
A sheet metal feature that combines a bend and a tab in a single operation.

Equation
Creates a mathematical relation between sketch dimensions, using dimension names as variables, or between feature parameters, such as the depth of an extruded feature or the instance count in a pattern.

Exploded view
Shows an assembly with its components separated from one another, usually to show how to assemble the mechanism.

Export
Save a SOLIDWORKS document in another format for use in other CAD/CAM, rapid prototyping, web, or graphics software applications.

Extension line
The line extending from the model indicating the point from which a dimension is measured.

Extrude
A feature that linearly projects a sketch to either add material to a part (in a base or boss) or remove material from a part (in a cut or hole).

Face
A selectable area (planar or otherwise) of a model or surface with boundaries that help define the shape of the model or surface. For example, a rectangular solid has six faces.

Fasteners
A SOLIDWORKS Toolbox library that adds fasteners automatically to holes in an assembly.

Feature
An individual shape that, combined with other features, makes up a part or assembly. Some features, such as bosses and cuts, originate as sketches. Other features, such as shells and fillets, modify a feature's geometry. However, not all features have associated geometry. Features are always listed in the FeatureManager design tree.

FeatureManager design tree
Located on the left side of the SOLIDWORKS window, it provides an outline view of the active part, assembly, or drawing.

Fill
A solid area hatch or crosshatch. Fill also applies to patches on surfaces.

Fillet
An internal rounding of a corner or edge in a sketch, or an edge on a surface or solid.

Forming tool
Dies that bend, stretch, or otherwise form sheet metal to create such form features as louvers, lances, flanges, and ribs.

Fully defined
A sketch where all lines and curves in the sketch, and their positions, are described by dimensions or relations, or both, and cannot be moved. Fully defined sketch entities are shown in black.

Geometric tolerance
A set of standard symbols that specify the geometric characteristics and dimensional requirements of a feature.

Graphics area
The area in the SOLIDWORKS window where the part, assembly, or drawing appears.

Guide curve
A 2D or 3D curve used to guide a sweep or loft.

Handle
An arrow, square, or circle that you can drag to adjust the size or position of an entity (a feature, dimension, or sketch entity, for example).

Helix
A curve defined by pitch, revolutions, and height. A helix can be used, for example, as a path for a swept feature cutting threads in a bolt.

Hem
A sheet metal feature that folds back at the edge of a part. A hem can be open, closed, double, or tear-drop.

HLR
(Hidden lines removed) a view mode in which all edges of the model that are not visible from the current view angle are removed from the display.

HLV
(Hidden lines visible) A view mode in which all edges of the model that are not visible from the current view angle are shown gray or dashed.

Import
Open files from other CAD software applications into a SOLIDWORKS document.

In-context feature
A feature with an external reference to the geometry of another component; the in-context feature changes automatically if the geometry of the referenced model or feature changes.

Inference
The system automatically creates (infers) relations between dragged entities (sketched entities, annotations, and components) and other entities and geometry. This is useful when positioning entities relative to one another.

Instance
An item in a pattern or a component in an assembly that occurs more than once. Blocks are inserted into drawings as instances of block definitions.

Interference detection
A tool that displays any interference between selected components in an assembly.

Jog
A sheet metal feature that adds material to a part by creating two bends from a sketched line.

Knit
A tool that combines two or more faces or surfaces into one. The edges of the surfaces must be adjacent and not overlapping, but they cannot ever be planar. There is no difference in the appearance of the face or the surface after knitting.

Layout sketch
A sketch that contains important sketch entities, dimensions, and relations. You reference the entities in the layout sketch when creating new sketches, building new geometry, or positioning components in an assembly. This allows for easier updating of your model because changes you make to the layout sketch propagate to the entire model.

Leader
A solid line from an annotation (note, dimension, and so on) to the referenced feature.

Library feature
A frequently used feature, or combination of features, that is created once and then saved for future use.

Lightweight
A part in an assembly or a drawing has only a subset of its model data loaded into memory. The remaining model data is loaded on an as-needed basis. This improves performance of large and complex assemblies.

Line
A straight sketch entity with two endpoints. A line can be created by projecting an external entity such as an edge, plane, axis, or sketch curve into the sketch.

Loft
A base, boss, cut, or surface feature created by transitions between profiles.

Lofted bend
A sheet metal feature that produces a roll form or a transitional shape from two open profile sketches. Lofted bends often create funnels and chutes.

Mass properties
A tool that evaluates the characteristics of a part or an assembly such as volume, surface area, centroid, and so on.

Mate
A geometric relationship, such as coincident, perpendicular, tangent, and so on, between parts in an assembly.

Mate reference
Specifies one or more entities of a component to use for automatic mating. When you drag a component with a mate reference into an assembly, the software tries to find other combinations of the same mate reference name and mate type.

Mates folder
A collection of mates that are solved together. The order in which the mates appear within the Mates folder does not matter.

Mirror
(a) A mirror feature is a copy of a selected feature, mirrored about a plane or planar face.
(b) A mirror sketch entity is a copy of a selected sketch entity that is mirrored about a centerline.

Miter flange
A sheet metal feature that joins multiple edge flanges together and miters the corner.

Model
3D solid geometry in a part or assembly document. If a part or assembly document contains multiple configurations, each configuration is a separate model.

Model dimension
A dimension specified in a sketch or a feature in a part or assembly document that defines some entity in a 3D model.

Model item
A characteristic or dimension of feature geometry that can be used in detailing drawings.

Model view
A drawing view of a part or assembly.

Mold
A set of manufacturing tooling used to shape molten plastic or other material into a designed part. You design the mold using a sequence of integrated tools that result in cavity and core blocks that are derived parts of the part to be molded.

Motion Study
Motion Studies are graphical simulations of motion and visual properties with assembly models. Analogous to a configuration, they do not actually change the original assembly model or its properties. They display the model as it changes based on simulation elements you add.

Multibody part
A part with separate solid bodies within the same part document. Unlike the components in an assembly, multibody parts are not dynamic.

Native format
DXF and DWG files remain in their original format (are not converted into SOLIDWORKS format) when viewed in SOLIDWORKS drawing sheets (view only).

Open profile
Also called an open contour, it is a sketch or sketch entity with endpoints exposed. For example, a U-shaped profile is open.

Ordinate dimensions
A chain of dimensions measured from a zero ordinate in a drawing or sketch.

Origin
The model origin appears as three gray arrows and represents the (0,0,0) coordinate of the model. When a sketch is active, a sketch origin appears in red and represents the (0,0,0) coordinate of the sketch. Dimensions and relations can be added to the model origin, but not to a sketch origin.

Out-of-context feature
A feature with an external reference to the geometry of another component that is not open.

Over defined
A sketch is over defined when dimensions or relations are either in conflict or redundant.

Parameter
A value used to define a sketch or feature (often a dimension).

Parent
An existing feature upon which other features depend. For example, in a block with a hole, the block is the parent to the child hole feature.

Part
A single 3D object made up of features. A part can become a component in an assembly, and it can be represented in 2D in a drawing. Examples of parts are bolt, pin, plate, and so on. The extension for a SOLIDWORKS part file name is .SLDPRT.

Path
A sketch, edge, or curve used in creating a sweep or loft.

Pattern
A pattern repeats selected sketch entities, features, or components in an array, which can be linear, circular, or sketch-driven. If the seed entity is changed, the other instances in the pattern update.

Physical Dynamics
An assembly tool that displays the motion of assembly components in a realistic way. When you drag a component, the component applies a force to other components it touches. Components move only within their degrees of freedom.

Pierce relation
Makes a sketch point coincident to the location at which an axis, edge, line, or spline pierces the sketch plane.

Planar
Entities that can lie on one plane. For example, a circle is planar, but a helix is not.

Plane
Flat construction geometry. Planes can be used for a 2D sketch, section view of a model, a neutral plane in a draft feature, and others.

Point
A singular location in a sketch, or a projection into a sketch at a single location of an external entity (origin, vertex, axis, or point in an external sketch).

Predefined view
A drawing view in which the view position, orientation, and so on can be specified before a model is inserted. You can save drawing documents with predefined views as templates.

Profile
A sketch entity used to create a feature (such as a loft) or a drawing view (such as a detail view). A profile can be open (such as a U shape or open spline) or closed (such as a circle or closed spline).

Projected dimension
If you dimension entities in an isometric view, projected dimensions are the flat dimensions in 2D.

Projected view
A drawing view projected orthogonally from an existing view.

PropertyManager
Located on the left side of the SOLIDWORKS window, it is used for dynamic editing of sketch entities and most features.

RealView graphics
A hardware (graphics card) support of advanced shading in real time; the rendering applies to the model and is retained as you move or rotate a part.

Rebuild
Tool that updates (or regenerates) the document with any changes made since the last time the model was rebuilt. Rebuild is typically used after changing a model dimension.

Reference dimension
A dimension in a drawing that shows the measurement of an item, but cannot drive the model and its value cannot be modified. When model dimensions change, reference dimensions update.

Reference geometry
Includes planes, axes, coordinate systems, and 3D curves. Reference geometry is used to assist in creating features such as lofts, sweeps, drafts, chamfers, and patterns.

Relation
A geometric constraint between sketch entities or between a sketch entity and a plane, axis, edge, or vertex. Relations can be added automatically or manually.

Relative view
A relative (or relative to model) drawing view is created relative to planar surfaces in a part or assembly.

Reload
Refreshes shared documents. For example, if you open a part file for read-only access while another user makes changes to the same part, you can reload the new version, including the changes.

Reorder
Reordering (changing the order of) items is possible in the FeatureManager design tree. In parts, you can change the order in which features are solved. In assemblies, you can control the order in which components appear in a bill of materials.

Replace
Substitutes one or more open instances of a component in an assembly with a different component.

Resolved
A state of an assembly component (in an assembly or drawing document) in which it is fully loaded in memory. All the component's model data is available, so its entities can be selected, referenced, edited, and used in mates, and so on.

Revolve
A feature that creates a base or boss, a revolved cut, or revolved surface by revolving one or more sketched profiles around a centerline.

Rip
A sheet metal feature that removes material at an edge to allow a bend.

Rollback
Suppresses all items below the rollback bar.

Section
Another term for profile in sweeps.

Section line
A line or centerline sketched in a drawing view to create a section view.

Section scope
Specifies the components to be left uncut when you create an assembly drawing section view.

Section view
A section view (or section cut) is (1) a part or assembly view cut by a plane, or (2) a drawing view created by cutting another drawing view with a section line.

Seed
A sketch or an entity (a feature, face, or body) that is the basis for a pattern. If you edit the seed, the other entities in the pattern are updated.

Shaded
Displays a model as a colored solid.

Shared values
Also called linked values, these are named variables that you assign to set the value of two or more dimensions to be equal.

Sheet format
Includes page size and orientation, standard text, borders, title blocks, and so on. Sheet formats can be customized and saved for future use. Each sheet of a drawing document can have a different format.

Shell
A feature that hollows out a part, leaving open the selected faces and thin walls on the remaining faces. A hollow part is created when no faces are selected to be open.

Sketch
A collection of lines and other 2D objects on a plane or face that forms the basis for a feature such as a base or a boss. A 3D sketch is non-planar and can be used to guide a sweep or loft, for example.

Smart Fasteners
Automatically adds fasteners (bolts and screws) to an assembly using the SOLIDWORKS Toolbox library of fasteners.

SmartMates
An assembly mating relation that is created automatically.

Solid sweep
A cut sweep created by moving a tool body along a path to cut out 3D material from a model.

Spiral
A flat or 2D helix, defined by a circle, pitch, and number of revolutions.

Spline
A sketched 2D or 3D curve defined by a set of control points.

Split line
Projects a sketched curve onto a selected model face, dividing the face into multiple faces so that each can be selected individually. A split line can be used to create draft features, to create face blend fillets, and to radiate surfaces to cut molds.

Stacked balloon
A set of balloons with only one leader. The balloons can be stacked vertically (up or down) or horizontally (left or right).

Standard 3 views
The three orthographic views (front, right, and top) that are often the basis of a drawing.

StereoLithography
The process of creating rapid prototype parts using a faceted mesh representation in STL files.

Sub-assembly
An assembly document that is part of a larger assembly. For example, the steering mechanism of a car is a sub-assembly of the car.

Suppress
Removes an entity from the display and from any calculations in which it is involved. You can suppress features, assembly components, and so on. Suppressing an entity does not delete the entity; you can un-suppress the entity to restore it.

Surface
A zero-thickness planar or 3D entity with edge boundaries. Surfaces are often used to create solid features. Reference surfaces can be used to modify solid features.

Sweep
Creates a base, boss, cut, or surface feature by moving a profile (section) along a path. For cut-sweeps, you can create solid sweeps by moving a tool body along a path.

Tangent arc
An arc that is tangent to another entity, such as a line.

Tangent edge
The transition edge between rounded or filleted faces in hidden lines visible or hidden lines removed modes in drawings.

Task Pane
Located on the right-side of the SOLIDWORKS window, the Task Pane contains SOLIDWORKS Resources, the Design Library, and the File Explorer.

Template
A document (part, assembly, or drawing) that forms the basis of a new document. It can include user-defined parameters, annotations, predefined views, geometry, and so on.

Temporary axis
An axis created implicitly for every conical or cylindrical face in a model.

Thin feature
An extruded or revolved feature with constant wall thickness. Sheet metal parts are typically created from thin features.

TolAnalyst
A tolerance analysis application that determines the effects that dimensions and tolerances have on parts and assemblies.

Top-down design
An assembly modeling technique where you create parts in the context of an assembly by referencing the geometry of other components. Changes to the referenced components propagate to the parts that you create in context.

Triad
Three axes with arrows defining the X, Y, and Z directions. A reference triad appears in part and assembly documents to assist in orienting the viewing of models. Triads also assist when moving or rotating components in assemblies.

Under defined
A sketch is under defined when there are not enough dimensions and relations to prevent entities from moving or changing size.

Vertex
A point at which two or more lines or edges intersect. Vertices can be selected for sketching, dimensioning, and many other operations.

Viewports
Windows that display views of models. You can specify one, two, or four viewports. Viewports with orthogonal views can be linked, which links orientation and rotation.

Virtual sharp
A sketch point at the intersection of two entities after the intersection itself has been removed by a feature such as a fillet or chamfer. Dimensions and relations to the virtual sharp are retained even though the actual intersection no longer exists.

Weldment
A multibody part with structural members.

Weldment cut list
A table that tabulates the bodies in a weldment along with descriptions and lengths.

Wireframe
A view mode in which all edges of the part or assembly are displayed.

Zebra stripes
Simulate the reflection of long strips of light on a very shiny surface. They allow you to see small changes in a surface that may be hard to see with a standard display.

Zoom
To simulate movement toward or away from a part or an assembly.

Index

1, 2, 3
1060 alloy, 3-9, 8-16
2-point spline, 6-5
3D sketch, 2-1, 2-3, 2-5, 2-6, 2-8, 2-13

A
abs, 8-21
advanced weldments, 2-1
alloy steel, 10-5
along X, 2-3
along Z, 2-3, 2-8
angle, 1-9
angular dimensions, 1-6, 1-7
annotation, 5-6
ansi inch, 2-8
ansi, 5-4, 10-3
assembly drawing, 5-1
assigning material, 3-9, 8-16, 8-21
auto relief, 3-6
axis, 6-3

B
balloons, 5-8
belt Chain, 1-1, 1-5, 1-10, 1-11, 1-12, 1-13, 1-17
belt length, 1-1, 1-13
belt, 1-4, 1-6, 1-7, 1-9, 1-10, 1-12, 1-13, 1-16
belts, 1-1
bend edges, 3-5
bend radius, 3-1
bill of materials, 5-1, 5-4, 5-6
blind, 3-8, 8-11
block, 1-4, 1-5, 1-7, 1-12
bom, 5-1, 5-2, 5-6, 5-8, 5-9
boss/base, 6-8, 7-4, 7-5, 7-9, 7-10
bottom up, 6-1
box-select, 1-4, 1-11, 1-12
Break Link, 9-10

C
calculating the mass, 2-12
cam part, 4-1
cam, 4-1, 4-2, 4-3, 4-4, 4-5, 4-6
cavity, 8-7
center of mass, 6-9, 10-6
centerline, 1-3
centerlines, 1-3, 1-7
center-rectangle, 7-3, 7-5, 8-12
circle, 6-7, 7-8, 7-10, 10-7, 10-8, 10-9
circles, 1-3, 1-4, 1-6, 1-11, 1-15
circular pattern, 8-20
circular spring, 10-7, 10-9
clearance, 6-1
click+hold+drag, 2-7
closed loop, 4-1, 4-4
coincident, 1-14, 6-4, 6-7
collect all bends, 3-5, 3-7, 3-8
color, 9-6, 9-7
column property, 5-7
column right, 5-6, 5-7
columns, 5-6
combine, 7-1, 7-6
combine-add, 7-1
combine-common, 7-1, 7-3, 7-6, 7-11
combine-subtract, 7-1
common, 7-1, 7-2, 7-6, 7-11
concentric, 6-4
configuration, 5-1
ConfigurationManager, 5-3
constant size, 8-14
constant thickness, 3-1
constrained, 6-6
constraint, 4-1, 4-4

convert Entities, 7-9
convert to sheet metal, 3-5
convert-entities, 8-7
copper pipe, 6-1
copper, 6-1, 6-2, 6-9
copy, 7-5
CSWE, 1-1
curve, 6-5
curved, 10-1, 10-6
custom properties, 5-1, 5-6
Cut with Surface, 9-5, 9-9, 9-10, 9-13
cylindrical, 4-1, 4-4

D

deactivate, 2-7
decimal places, 10-6
define, 10-5
degrees of freedom, 4-3
delete and Patch, 8-8, 8-9, 8-10
delete Face, 8-8, 8-9, 8-10
design intent, 6-1, 8-1
dimensions, 2-4, 2-6, 2-7, 2-13, 8-1, 8-11, 8-12, 8-19, 10-3, 10-4
display style, 3-4
Display, 9-7
document, 3-1, 3-3, 3-4
drafting standards, 10-3
drag and drop, 5-5
drawing template, 5-4
drawing view, 5-1, 5-5, 5-6
driven, 1-7
driving dimension, 1-8
driving, 1-1, 1-3, 1-7, 1-8

E

Edit Component, 9-8
edit material, 10-5
Edit Part, 9-3, 9-7
editing, 9-9
end point, 6-7
equal spacing, 8-20

errors, 8-6
evaluate, 3-5, 3-6, 3-9, 4-5, 6-9, 7-7, 7-12, 8-4, 8-17, 8-21, 9-8
evaluation, 10-6
exam preparation, 1-1
exploded view, 9-3
extruded bodies, 7-6, 7-11
extruded boss/base, 8-8
extruded cut, 3-8, 8-13, 8-19

F

feature tree, 6-3, 6-4, 6-9, 8-20
FeatureManager, 1-5, 1-15, 10-5
features history, 9-9
features, 6-8, 7-4, 7-6, 7-9, 7-10, 7-11, 8-8, 8-11, 8-13, 8-14, 8-15, 8-19, 10-4
Fillet, 9-7
final mass, 8-17
finish, 5-8
fit spline, 6-6
fittings, 6-1
fixed face, 3-1, 3-5, 3-7, 3-8
flat length, 3-6
Flip Cut, 9-5
flip direction, 1-6
flip Side To Cut, 8-13, 8-19
fold, 3-7, 3-8
front plane, 1-3, 1-11
fully constrained, 6-3
fully define, 7-4, 7-8, 7-9, 7-10, 8-11, 8-12, 8-19, 10-3, 10-7
fully defined, 4-3, 7-4

G

gap, 3-5
geometry, 8-1, 8-6, 9-3
graphics, 9-5, 9-6, 9-7

H

handles, 6-5
heads-up view, 3-4, 8-15

Hide Component, 9-6
Hide, 9-6, 9-12, 10-9
hide/show, 6-3
Hiding, 9-6, 9-12
horizontal, 10-7, 10-8

I
IGES, 3-1, 3-3, 3-4
import free points, 5-4
in context, 6-1
inactive, 9-3, 9-7
Inch, Pound, Second, 1-3
indented, 5-1, 5-9
inplace, 6-4
insert component, 6-4
Insert Part, 9-10
insert, 5-6, 5-7, 7-6, 7-11
insertion point, 1-4, 1-5, 1-12
intersected, 10-1
IPS, 1-3, 10-3
isometric, 2-7
item numbers, 5-1

J
join, 7-1

L
landscape, 5-4
layout sketch, 6-1
line, 2-3, 2-7, 6-4, 6-7
link to thickness, 5-8

M
make block, 1-4, 1-11, 1-12
manipulate, 6-5
mass properties, 5-9
mass Property, 7-7, 7-12
mass, 2-9, 2-10, 2-12, 2-14, 8-1, 8-4, 8-16, 8-17, 8-18, 8-21, 10-6
mate, 4-4

material, 2-9, 6-1, 6-9, 8-16, 8-21, 10-5, 10-6
maximum distance, 4-1
measure, 4-5, 4-6, 5-6
merge result, 7-5, 7-10, 8-11
mid plane, 7-4, 7-9, 7-10
minimized, 10-1
minimum distance, 4-5
modifications, 8-1, 8-3, 8-6, 8-18
modifying, 2-13
mold, 8-6, 8-17
motor, 6-3, 6-10
Move/Copy, 9-10
multibody parts, 8-18, 8-22
multibody, 7-1, 7-6, 9-11
multiple bodies, 7-1, 7-6
multiple solid, 7-1

N
new component, 6-3, 6-4
new group, 2-8, 2-11
new Part, 6-4
new sketch, 6-4, 6-7, 7-3, 7-5, 7-8, 7-10
no numbering, 5-9
normal distance, 5-6
number of turn, 10-5, 10-8

O
offset distance, 7-4, 7-9, 9-4
offset entities, 7-4
offset, 7-9
Offset-Surface, 9-3
open butt, 5-5
option, 3-3
options, 10-6
orientation, 10-5, 10-8
origin, 1-3, 1-14, 10-3, 10-4
over defined, 1-7
overlapping, 7-1, 9-6
overlaps, 3-5

P

pan icon, 5-9
part number, 5-7, 5-8
part template, 1-3, 10-3
parts only, 5-1, 5-6
patching, 8-1
path, 10-1, 10-2, 10-3
pattern angle, 8-4, 8-5
pattern, 8-4, 8-5, 8-20
performance, 8-3
pierce relation, 10-7, 10-8
pipe, 2-8, 2-11
planar faces, 8-8
plane, 10-3, 10-4
plastics, 8-21
pop-up menu, 9-12
preview, 7-6, 7-11
profile, 8-11, 8-19, 10-1, 10-2, 10-3, 10-4
properties, 5-1, 5-4, 10-6
property name, 5-7, 5-8
pulley, 1-4, 1-6, 1-9
pulleys, 1-1, 1-2

Q

quantity, 5-4, 5-7

R

radius, 9-7
rebuild, 1-8, 1-9, 1-14, 1-16, 8-4, 8-5
rectangular, 3-6
reference geometry, 6-3
relations, 1-1, 8-11, 8-19, 10-3
repair, 8-6
Reverse, 9-11
revolve, 8-11
rips, 3-1
rotation, 8-15

S

scale, 5-4
section view, 8-15
select-tangency, 8-7, 9-4, 9-7
shaded mode, 3-4
shaded with edges, 3-4
sheet metal parameters, 3-1
sheet metal tools, 3-5
shell, 8-15
sketch entities, 1-5, 1-13
sketch, 8-7, 8-11, 8-12, 8-19, 10-3, 10-4
smart dimension, 1-15
solid body, 7-3, 7-5, 7-8, 7-9, 7-10
solid model, 9-5, 9-9, 9-10, 9-11, 9-12
spline, 6-5, 6-6, 6-7
structural members, 2-1, 2-8
sub-assemblies, 5-1, 5-3
sub-component, 5-9
Suppressing, 9-6
surface area, 10-6
surface model, 9-4, 9-5, 9-6, 9-9, 9-10, 9-11, 9-12
surfaces, 8-8
sw-configuration name, 5-7
sweep path, 6-8, 10-4, 10-7, 10-8, 10-9
sweep profile, 6-8, 10-4, 10-7, 10-8, 10-9
sweep, 6-7, 6-8, 10-3, 10-4
swept boss/base, 10-4, 10-9
swept surface, 10-8, 10-9

T

tab key, 2-3
tables, 5-6
tangent mate, 4-1, 4-4
tangent relation, 6-5
teeth, 4-1
temporary Axis, 6-3
thickness, 3-1, 3-5, 8-15
thin, 10-1
third angle, 5-4
through all, 8-13, 8-19
title block, 5-5
tolerance, 6-6
tools, 6-6

top level, 5-1
top plane, 2-5
top-down assembly, 6-3
trim order, 2-1, 2-11
trim/extend, 2-1
turns, 10-5
twist along path, 10-4, 10-8
twist type, 10-4, 10-8
twisting, 10-1

U
unfold, 3-7
unsuppressed, 8-3
updating, 8-1
use custom settings, 10-6

V
view palette, 5-5
virtual intersection, 8-16
volume
volume, 7-1, 7-7, 7-12, 10-6

W
weldment corner, 2-1
wheel, 4-1, 4-4, 4-5, 4-6

Z
z direction, 2-3

SOLIDWORKS Quick Guide

Quick Reference Guide to SOLIDWORKS Command Icons & Toolbars

STANDARD Toolbar

	Creates a new document.			Loads or unloads the 3D instant website add-in
	Opens an existing document.			Select tool.
	Saves an active document.			Select the entire document.
	Make Drawing from Part/Assembly			Checks read-only files.
	Make Assembly from Part/Assembly			Options.
	Prints the active document.			Help
	Print preview			Full screen view.
	Cuts the selection & puts it on the clipboard.			OK.
	Copies the selection & puts it on the clipboard.			Cancel.
	Inserts the clipboard contents.			Magnified selection.
	Deletes the selection.			
	Reverses the last action.			
	Rebuilds the part / assembly / drawing.			

SKETCH TOOLS Toolbar

	Redo the last action that was undone.	
	Saves all documents.	
	Edits material.	
	Closes an existing document	
	Shows or hides the Selection Filter toolbar.	
	Shows or hides the Web toolbar.	
	Properties.	
	File properties	

Select
Sketch
3D Sketch
Sketches a rectangle from the center.
Sketches a centerpoint arc slot.
Sketches a 3-point arc slot.
Sketches a straight slot.
Sketches a centerpoint straight slot.
Sketches a 3-point arc.
Creates sketched ellipses.

Quick Reference Guide to SOLIDWORKS Command Icons & Toolbars

SKETCH TOOLS Toolbar

Icon	Description
	3D sketch on plane.
	Sets up Grid parameters.
	Creates a sketch on a selected plane or face.
	Equation driven curve
	Modifies a sketch.
	Copies sketch entities.
	Scales sketch entities.
	Rotates sketch entities.
	Sketches 3 point rectangle from the center.
	Sketches 3 point corner rectangle.
	Sketches a line.
	Creates a center point arc: center, start, end.
	Creates an arc tangent to a line.
	Sketches splines on a surface or face.
	Sketches a circle.
	Sketches a circle by its perimeter.
	Makes a path of sketch entities.
	Mirrors entities dynamically about a
	Insert a plane into the 3D sketch.
	Instant 2D.
	Sketch numeric input.
	Detaches segment on drag.
	Sketch picture
	Partial ellipses.
	Adds a Parabola.
	Adds a spline.
	Sketches a polygon.
	Sketches a corner rectangle.
	Sketches a parallelogram.
	Creates points.
	Creates sketched centerlines.
	Adds text to sketch.
	Converts selected model edges or sketch entities to sketch segments.
	Creates a sketch along the intersection of multiple bodies.
	Converts face curves on the selected face into 3D sketch entities.
	Mirrors selected segments about a centerline.
	Fillets the corner of two lines.
	Creates a chamfer between two sketch entities.
	Creates a sketch curve by offsetting model edges or sketch entities at a specified distance.
	Trims a sketch segment.
	Extends a sketch segment.
	Splits a sketch segment.
	Construction Geometry.
	Creates linear steps and repeat of sketch entities.
	Creates circular steps and repeat of sketch entities.

Quick Reference Guide to SOLIDWORKS Command Icons & Toolbars

SHEET METAL Toolbar

 Add a bend from a selected sketch in a Sheet Metal part.

 Shows flat pattern for this sheet metal part.

 Shows part without inserting any bends.

 Inserts a rip feature to a sheet metal part.

 Create a Sheet Metal part or add material to existing Sheet Metal part

 Inserts a Sheet Metal Miter Flange feature.

 Folds selected bends.

 Unfolds selected bends.

 Inserts bends using a sketch line.

 Inserts a flange by pulling an edge.

 Inserts a sheet metal corner feature.

 Inserts a Hem feature by selecting edges.

 Breaks a corner by filleting/chamfering it.

 Inserts a Jog feature using a sketch line.

 Inserts a lofted bend feature using 2 sketches.

 Creates inverse dent on a sheet metal part.

 Trims out material from a corner, in a sheet metal

 Inserts a fillet weld bead.

 Converts a solid/surface into a sheet metal part.

 Adds a Cross Break feature into a selected face.

 Sweeps an open profile along an open/closed path.

 Adds a gusset/rib across a bend

 Corner relief

 Welds the selected corner

SURFACES Toolbar

 Creates mid surfaces between offset face pairs.

 Patches surface holes and external edges.

 Creates an extruded surface.

 Creates a revolved surface.

 Creates a swept surface.

 Creates a lofted surface.

 Creates an offset surface.

 Radiates a surface originating from a curve, parallel to a plane.

 Knits surfaces together.

 Creates a planar surface from a sketch or A set of edges.

 Creates a surface by importing data from a file.

 Extends a surface.

 Trims a surface.

 Surface flatten

 Deletes Face(s).

 Replaces Face with Surface.

 Patches surface holes and external edges by extending the surfaces.

 Creates parting surfaces between core & cavity surfaces.

 Inserts ruled surfaces from edges.

WELDMENTS Toolbar

 Creates a weldment feature.

 Creates a structure member feature.

 Adds a gusset feature between 2 planar adjoining faces.

 Creates an end cap feature.

 Adds a fillet weld bead feature.

 Trims or extends structure members.

 Weld bead.

Quick Reference Guide to SOLIDWORKS Command Icons & Toolbars

DIMENSIONS/RELATIONS Toolbar

 Inserts dimension between two lines.

 Creates a horizontal dimension between selected entities.

 Creates a vertical dimension between selected entities.

 Creates a reference dimension between selected entities.

 Creates a set of ordinate dimensions.

 Creates a set of Horizontal ordinate dimensions.

 Creates a set of Vertical ordinate dimensions.

 Creates a chamfer dimension.

 Adds a geometric relation.

 Automatically Adds Dimensions to the current sketch.

 Displays and deletes geometric relations.

 Fully defines a sketch.

 Scans a sketch for elements of equal length or radius.

 Angular Running dimension

 Display / Delete dimension.

 Isolate changed dimension.

 Path length dimension.

BLOCK Toolbar

 Makes a new block.

 Edits the selected block.

 Inserts a new block to a sketch or drawing.

 Adds/Removes sketch entities to/from blocks.

 Updates parent sketches effected by this block.

 Saves the block to a file.

 Explodes the selected block.

 Inserts a belt.

STANDARD VIEWS Toolbar

 Front view.

 Back view.

 Left view.

 Right view.

 Top view.

 Bottom view.

 Isometric view.

 Trimetric view.

 Dimetric view.

 Normal to view.

 Links all views in the viewport together.

 Displays viewport with front & right views

 Displays a 4 view viewport with 1st or 3rd Angle of projection.

 Displays viewport with front & top

 Displays viewport with a single

 View selector.

 New view.

FEATURES Toolbar

 Creates a boss feature by extruding a sketched profile.

 Creates a revolved feature based on profile and angle parameter.

 Creates a cut feature by extruding a sketched profile.

 Creates a cut feature by revolving a sketched profile.

 Thread

 Creates a cut by sweeping a closed profile along an open or closed path.

 Loft cut

 Creates a cut by thickening one or more adjacent surfaces.

 Adds a deformed surface by push or pull on i

 Creates a lofted feature between two or more profiles.

 Creates a solid feature by thickening one or more adjacent surfaces.

 Creates a filled feature.

 Chamfers an edge or a chain of tangent edges.

 Inserts a rib feature.

 Combine.

 Creates a shell feature.

 Applies draft to a selected surface.

 Creates a cylindrical hole.

 Inserts a hole with a pre-defined cross section.

 Puts a dome surface on a face.

 Model break view.

 Applies global deformation to solid or surface bodies.

 Wraps closed sketch contour(s) onto a face.

 Curve Driven pattern.

 Suppresses the selected feature or component.

 Un-suppresses the selected feature or component.

 Flexes solid and surface bodies

 Intersect

 Variable Patterns

 Live Section Plane

 Mirrors.

 Scale.

 Creates a Sketch Driven pattern.

 Creates a Table Driven Pattern.

 Inserts a split Feature.

 Hole series.

 Joins bodies from one or more parts into a single part in the context of an assembly.

 Deletes a solid or a surface.

 Instant 3D

 Inserts a part from file into the active part document.

 Moves/Copies solid and surface bodies or moves graphics bodies.

 Merges short edges on faces

 Pushes solid / surface model by another solid / surface model

 Moves face(s) of a solid

 FeatureWorks Options.

 Linear Pattern.

 Fill Pattern.

 Cuts a solid model with a surface.

 Boundary Boss/Base

 Boundary Cut

 Circular Pattern

 Recognize Features

 Grid System

MOLD TOOLS Toolbar

 Extracts core(s) from existing tooling split

 Constructs a surface patch

 Moves face(s) of a solid

 Creates offset surfaces.

 Inserts cavity into a base part.

 Scales a model by a specified factor.

 Applies draft to a selected surface.

 Inserts a split line feature.

 Creates parting lines to separate core & cavity surfaces

 Finds & creates mold shut-off surfaces

 Creates a planar surface from a sketch or a set of edges.

 Knits surfaces together.

 Inserts ruled surfaces from edges.

 Creates parting surfaces between core & cavity surfaces

 Creates multiple bodies from a single body.

 Inserts a tooling split feature.

 Creates parting surfaces between the core & cavity.

 Inserts surface body folders for mold operation.

SELECTION FILTERS Toolbar

 Turns selection filters on and off.

 Clears all filters.

 Selects all filters.

 Inverts current selection.

 Allows selection of edges only.

 Allows selection filter for vertices only.

 Allows selection of faces only.

 Adds filter for Surface Bodies.

 Adds filter for Solid Bodies.

 Adds filter for Axes.

 Adds filter for Planes.

 Adds filter for Sketch Points.

 Allows selection for sketch only.

 Adds filter for Sketch Segments.

 Adds filter for Midpoints.

 Adds filter for Center Marks.

 Adds filter for Centerline.

 Adds filter for Dimensions and Hole Callouts.

 Adds filter for Surface Finish Symbols.

 Adds filter for Geometric Tolerances.

 Adds filter for Notes / Balloons.

 Adds filter for Weld Symbols.

 Adds filter for Weld beads.

 Adds filter for Datum Targets.

 Adds filter for Datum feature only.

 Adds filter for blocks.

 Adds filter for Cosmetic Threads.

Adds filter for Dowel pin symbols.

 Adds filter for connection points.

 Adds filter for routing points.

SOLIDWORKS Add-Ins Toolbar

 Loads/unloads CircuitWorks add-in.

 Loads/unloads the Design Checker add-in.

 Loads/unloads the PhotoView 360 add-in.

 Loads/unloads the Scan-to-3D add-in.

 Loads/unloads the SOLIDWORKS Motions add-in.

 Loads/unloads the SOLIDWORKS Routing add-in.

 Loads/unloads the SOLIDWORKS Simulation add-in.

 Loads/unloads the SOLIDWORKS Toolbox add-in.

 Loads/unloads the SOLIDWORKS TolAnalysis add-in.

 Loads/unloads the SOLIDWORKS Flow Simulation add-in.

 Loads/unloads the SOLIDWORKS Plastics add-in.

 Loads/unloads the SOLIDWORKS MBD SNL license.

FASTENING FEATURES Toolbar

 Creates a parameterized mounting boss.

 Creates a parameterized snap hook.

 Creates a groove to mate with a hook feature.

 Uses sketch elements to create a vent for air flow.

 Creates a lip/groove feature.

SCREEN CAPTURE Toolbar

 Copies the current graphics window to the clipboard.

 Records the current graphics window to an AVI file.

 Stops recording the current graphics window to an AVI file.

EXPLODE LINE SKETCH Toolbar

 Adds a route line that connect entities.

 Adds a jog to the route lines.

LINE FORMAT Toolbar

 Changes layer properties.

 Changes the current document layer.

 Changes line color.

 Changes line thickness.

 Changes line style.

 Hides / Shows a hidden edge.

 Changes line display mode.

 Did you know??
* Ctrl+Q will force a rebuild on all features of a part.
* Ctrl+B will rebuild the feature being worked on and its dependants.

2D-To-3D Toolbar

 Makes a Front sketch from the selected entities.

 Makes a Top sketch from the selected entities.

 Makes a Right sketch from the selected entities.

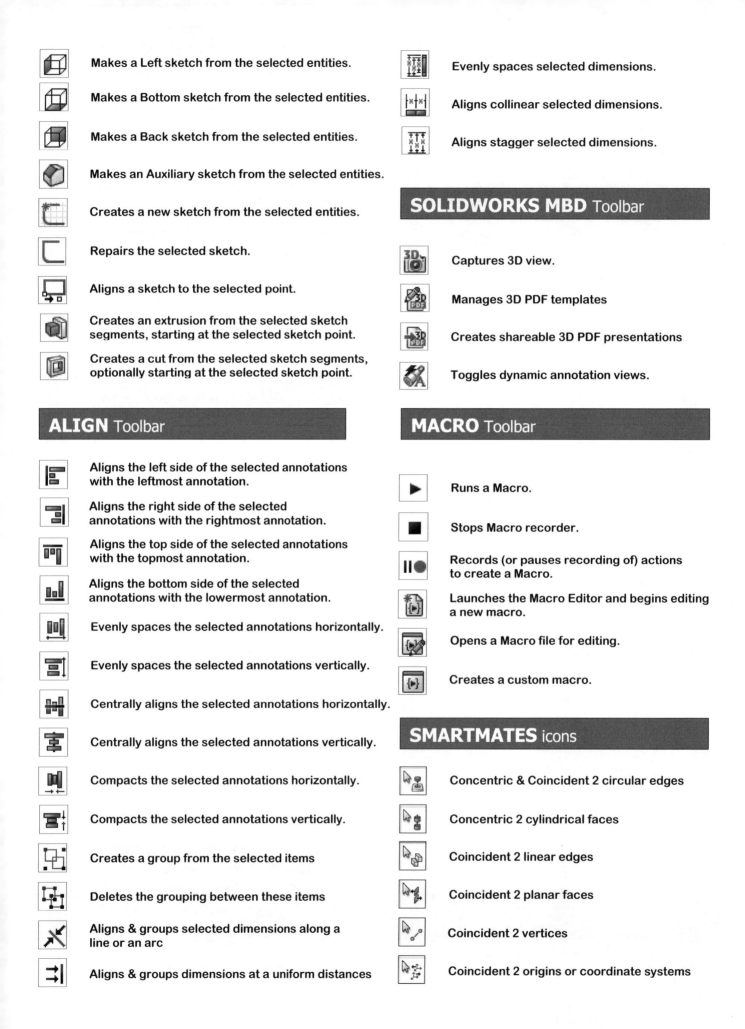

TABLE Toolbar

 Adds a hole table of selected holes from a specified origin datum.

 Adds a Bill of Materials.

 Adds a revision table.

 Displays a Design table in a drawing.

 Adds a weldments cuts list table.

 Adds a Excel based of Bill of Materials

 Adds a weldment cut list table

REFERENCE GEOMETRY Toolbar

 Adds a reference plane

 Creates an axis.

 Creates a coordinate system.

 Adds the center of mass.

 Specifies entities to use as references using SmartMates.

SPLINE TOOLS Toolbar

 Inserts a point to a spline.

 Displays all points where the concavity of selected spline changes.

 Displays minimum radius of selected spline.

 Displays curvature combs of selected spline.

 Reduces numbers of points in a selected spline.

 Adds a tangency control.

 Adds a curvature control.

 Adds a spline based on selected sketch entities & edges.

 Displays the spline control polygon.

ANNOTATIONS Toolbar

 Inserts a note.

 Inserts a surface finish symbol.

 Inserts a new geometric tolerancing symbol.

 Attaches a balloon to the selected edge or face.

 Adds balloons for all components in selected view.

 Inserts a stacked balloon.

 Attaches a datum feature symbol to a selected edge / detail.

 Inserts a weld symbol on the selected edge / face / vertex.

 Inserts a datum target symbol and / or point attached to a selected edge / line.

 Selects and inserts block.

 Inserts annotations & reference geometry from the part / assembly into the selected.

 Adds center marks to circles on model.

 Inserts a Centerline.

 Inserts a hole callout.

 Adds a cosmetic thread to the selected cylindrical feature.

 Inserts a Multi-Jog leader.

 Selects a circular edge or and arc for Dowel pin symbol insertion.

 Adds a view location symbol.

 Inserts latest version symbol.

 Adds a cross hatch patterns or solid fill.

 Adds a weld bead caterpillar on an edge.

 Adds a weld symbol on a selected entity.

 Inserts a revision cloud.

 Inserts a magnetic line.

 Hides/shows annotation.

DRAWINGS Toolbar

 Updates the selected view to the model's current stage.

 Creates a detail view.

 Creates a section view.

 Inserts an Alternate Position view.

 Unfolds a new view from an existing view.

 Generates a standard 3-view drawing (1st or 3rd angle).

 Inserts an auxiliary view of an inclined surface.

 Adds an Orthogonal or Named view based on an existing part or assembly.

 Adds a Relative view by two orthogonal faces or planes.

 Adds a Predefined orthogonal projected or Named view with a model.

 Adds an empty view.

 Adds vertical break lines to selected view.

 Crops a view.

 Creates a Broken-out section.

QUICK SNAP Toolbar

 Snap to points.

 Snap to center points.

 Snap to midpoints.

 Snap to quadrant points.

 Snap to intersection of 2 curves.

 Snap to nearest curve.

 Snap tangent to curve.

 Snap perpendicular to curve.

 Snap parallel to line.

 Snap horizontally / vertically to points.

 Snap horizontally / vertically.

 Snap to discrete line lengths.

 Snap to angle.

LAYOUT Toolbar

 Creates the assembly layout sketch.

 Sketches a line.

 Sketches a corner rectangle.

 Sketches a circle.

 Sketches a 3 point arc.

 Rounds a corner.

 Trims or extends a sketch.

 Adds sketch entities by offsetting faces, Edges curves.

 Mirrors selected entities about a centerline.

 Adds a relation.

 Creates a dimension.

 Displays / Deletes geometric relations.

 Makes a new block.

 Edits the selected block.

 Inserts a new block to the sketch or drawing.

 Adds / Removes sketch entities to / from a block.

 Saves the block to a file.

 Explodes the selected block.

 Creates a new part from a layout sketch block.

Positions 2 components relative to one another.

CURVES Toolbar

 Projects sketch onto selected surface.

 Inserts a split line feature.

 Creates a composite curve from selected edges, curves and sketches.

 Creates a curve through free points.

 Creates a 3D curve through reference points.

 Helical curve defined by a base sketch and shape parameters.

VIEW Toolbar

 Displays a view in the selected orientation.

 Reverts to previous view.

 Redraws the current window.

 Zooms out to see entire model.

 Zooms in by dragging a bounding box.

 Zooms in or out by dragging up or down.

 Zooms to fit all selected entities.

 Dynamic view rotation.

 Scrolls view by dragging.

 Displays image in wireframe mode.

 Displays hidden edges in gray.

 Displays image with hidden lines removed.

 Controls the visibility of planes.

 Controls the visibility of axis.

 Controls the visibility of parting lines.

 Controls the visibility of temporary axis.

 Controls the visibility of origins.

 Controls the visibility of coordinate systems.

 Controls the visibility of reference curves.

 Controls the visibility of sketches.

 Controls the visibility of 3D sketch planes.

 Controls the visibility of 3D sketch

 Controls the visibility of all annotations.

 Controls the visibility of reference points.

 Controls the visibility of routing points.

 Controls the visibility of lights.

 Controls the visibility of cameras.

 Controls the visibility of sketch relations.

 Changes the display state for the current configuration.

 Rolls the model view.

 Turns the orientation of the model view.

 Dynamically manipulate the model view in 3D to make selection.

 Changes the display style for the active view.

 Displays a shade view of the model with its edges.

 Displays a shade view of the model.

 Toggles between draft quality & high quality HLV.

 Cycles through or applies a specific scene.

 Views the models through one of the model's cameras.

 Displays a part or assembly w/different colors according to the local radius of curvature.

 Displays zebra stripes.

 Displays a model with hardware accelerated shades.

 Applies a cartoon affect to model edges & faces

 Views simulations symbols

TOOLS Toolbar

 Calculates the distance between selected items.

 Adds or edits equation.

 Calculates the mass properties of the model.

 Checks the model for geometry errors.

 Inserts or edits a Design Table.

 Evaluates section properties for faces and sketches that lie in parallel planes.

 Reports Statistics for this Part/Assembly.

 Deviation Analysis.

 Runs the SimulationXpress analysis wizard Powered by SOLIDWORKS Simulation.

 Checks the spelling.

 Import diagnostics.

 Runs the DFMXpress analysis wizard.

 Runs the SOLIDWORKSFloXpress analysis wizard.

ASSEMBLY Toolbar

 Creates a new part & inserts it into the assembly.

 Adds an existing part or sub-assembly to the assembly.

 Creates a new assembly & inserts it into the assembly.

 Turns on/off large assembly mode for this document.

 Hides / shows model(s) associated with the selected model(s).

 Toggles the transparency of components.

 Changes the selected components to suppressed or resolved.

 Inserts a belt.

 Toggles between editing part and assembly.

 Smart Fasteners.

 Positions two components relative to one another.

 External references will not be created.

 Moves a component.

 Rotates an un-mated component around its center point.

 Replaces selected components.

 Replaces mate entities of mates of the selected components on the selected Mates group.

 Creates a New Exploded view.

 Creates or edits explode line sketch.

 Interference detection.

 Shows or Hides the Simulation toolbar.

 Patterns components in one or two linear directions.

 Patterns components around an axis.

 Sets the transparency of the components other than the one being edited

 Sketch driven component pattern.

 Pattern driven component pattern.

 Curve driven component pattern

 Chain driven component pattern

 SmartMates by dragging & dropping components

 Checks assembly hole alignments.

 Mirrors subassemblies and parts.

To add or remove an icon
to or from the toolbar, first select:

Tools/Customize/Commands

Next, select a **Category**, click a button to see its description and then drag/drop the command icon into any toolbar.

SOLIDWORKS Quick-Guide©
STANDARD Keyboard Shortcuts

Rotate the model

* Horizontally or Vertically: _____ Arrow keys
* Horizontally or Vertically 90°: _____ Shift + Arrow keys
* Clockwise or Counterclockwise: _____ Alt + left or right Arrow
* Pan the model: _____ Ctrl + Arrow keys
* Zoom in: _____ Z (shift + Z or capital Z)
* Zoom out: _____ z (lower case z)
* Zoom to fit: _____ F
* Previous view: _____ Ctrl+Shift+Z

View Orientation

* View Orientation Menu: _____ Space bar
* Front: _____ Ctrl+1
* Back: _____ Ctrl+2
* Left: _____ Ctrl+3
* Right: _____ Ctrl+4
* Top: _____ Ctrl+5
* Bottom: _____ Ctrl+6
* Isometric: _____ Ctrl+7

Selection Filter & Misc.

* Filter Edges: _____ e
* Filter Vertices: _____ v
* Filter Faces: _____ x
* Toggle Selection filter toolbar: _____ F5
* Toggle Selection Filter toolbar (on/off): _____ F6
* New SOLIDWORKS document: _____ F1
* Open Document: _____ Ctrl+O
* Open from Web folder: _____ Ctrl+W
* Save: _____ Ctrl+S
* Print: _____ Ctrl+P
* Magnifying Glass Zoom _____ g
* Switch between the SOLIDWORKS documents _____ Ctrl + Tab

SOLIDWORKS Quick-Guide©
Sample Customized Keyboard Shortcuts

SOLIDWORKS Sample Customized Hot Keys

Function Keys

F1	SW-Help
F2	2D Sketch
F3	3D Sketch
F4	Modify
F5	Selection Filters
F6	Move (2D Sketch)
F7	Rotate (2D Sketch)
F8	Measure
F9	Extrude
F10	Revolve
F11	Sweep
F12	Loft

Sketch

C	Circle
P	Polygon
E	Ellipse
O	Offset Entities
Alt + C	Convert Entities
M	Mirror
Alt + M	Dynamic Mirror
Alt + F	Sketch Fillet
T	Trim
Alt + X	Extend
D	Smart Dimension
Alt + R	Add Relation
Alt + P	Plane
Control + F	Fully Define Sketch
Control + Q	Exit Sketch

Quick-Guide, Part of SOLIDWORKS Basic Tools, Intermediate Skills and Advanced Techniques

SOLIDWORKS Quick-Guide by Paul Tran – Sr. Certified SOLIDWORKS Instructor
Issue 12 / Jan-2017 - Printed in The United State of America – All Rights Reserved